C. J. Childs

Brodie's Notes on E. M. Forster's

A Passage to India

Pan Books London, Sydney and Auckland

First published by James Brodie Ltd
This edition published 1976 by Pan Books Ltd
Cavaye Place, London SW10 9PG
9 8

ISBN 0 330 50183 6
Phototypeset by Input Typesetting Ltd, London SW19 8DR
Printed and bound in Great Britain by
Richard Clay Ltd, Bungay, Suffolk

Contents

Page references in these Notes are to the Penguin edition of *A Passage to India*, but references are also given to particular chapters, so that the Notes may be used with any edition of the novel.

To the student

A close reading of the set book is the student's primary task. These Notes will help to increase your understanding and appreciation of the novel, and to stimulate *your own* thinking about it; *they are in no way intended as a substitute* for a thorough knowledge of the book.

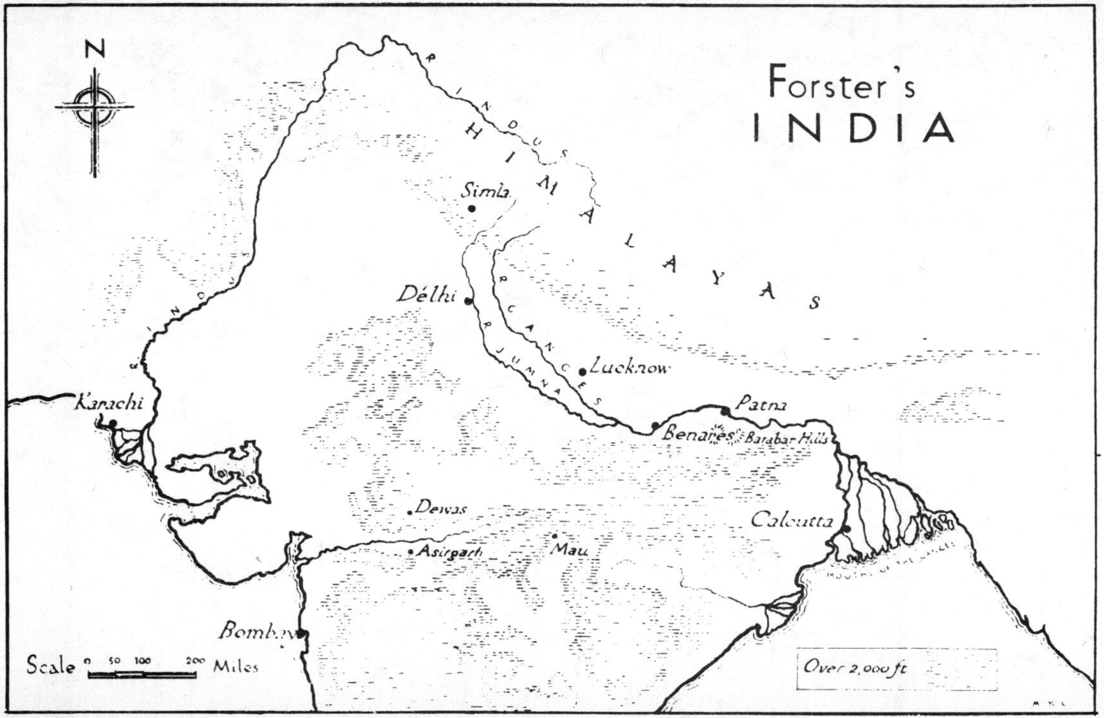
Forster's
INDIA
N
R. INDUS
HIMALAYAS
Simla
Délhi
R. GANGES
R. JUMNA
Lucknow
Patna
Benares
Barabar Hills
Karachi
Dewas
Asirgarh
Mau
Calcutta
Bombay
Scale 0 50 100 200 Miles
Over 2,000 ft

The author and his work

Edward Morgan Forster was born on 1 January 1879, at 6 Melcombe Place, Dorset Square, London. His father, also Edward Morgan, was the son of the Rev Charles Forster and his wife Laura (there were ten children). By his marriage Forster's grandfather had allied himself to the Thornton family, notable members of what has been called the 'intellectual aristocracy' of the English upper-middle classes. Originally members of the so-called Clapham sect of wealthy Evangelicals, their money, intellect and religious fervour had operated in compassionate, public-spirited and rigidly limited ways. In his essay 'Battersea Rise' (reprinted in *Abinger Harvest*) Forster describes this part of his heritage: 'Riches, evangelical piety, genuine goodness, narrowness, complacency, integrity, censoriousness, clannishness and a noble public spirit managed to flourish together in its ample bosom without mutual discomfort. No dancing and no cards; but heaps of food.'

Forster's mother, Alice Clara Whichelo, came, it seems, from quite a different family. In *Marianne Thornton*, the biography of his great-aunt, Forster describes them thus: they had 'no enthusiasm for work, they were devoid of public spirit, and they were averse to piety and quick to detect the falsity sometimes accompanying it.' His maternal grandmother, 'most amusing and witty, fond of pleasure, generous and improvident', Forster adored. The father, a drawing-master with 'the delicacy and the inclinations of a creative artist', had died suddenly, leaving his wife with ten children (Alice, called Lily, the eldest) and no money. The family muddled through. Forster remained friends with his grandmother: indeed 'It is with her – with them [the Whichelos] – that my heart lies.'

Forster's father died when the novelist was an infant,

but the connection with the Thorntons was maintained. Alice Clara Whichelo had been, in fact, a protégé of the Thorntons, and Forster himself became one of their especial concerns. The last section of *Marianne Thornton* contains loving reminiscences of Forster's very early life: the odious nickname he was given of 'The Important One'; the rather unsuccessful breakfast game his great-aunt, then in her eighties, tried to play with him; the Hertfordshire house where his mother settled, which he took to his heart – and which figures in *Howard's End*, that novel so impregnated with a sense of place. And the 'long stories' he used to fabricate 'about things that never happened except inside my head'; the maid Emmy who was such a suitable and uproarious companion, but who 'had to go'; the boy Ansell, 'reliable but not too reliable', who 'probably did more than anyone in armouring me against life'. This, he says, was 'an idyllic life'.

Then followed 'a snobbish Irish tutor who prepared me for a preparatory school which was to prepare me for the world'. The book closes with Forster's acknowledgment of another, more concrete, indebtedness to his Thornton ancestry: his great-aunt left him £8,000, the basis of the financial independence he enjoyed in the years up to about 1920, by which time the value of the bequest had diminished and his novels had begun to sell.

The Public School was Tonbridge. The school, or the place, figures in two of Forster's novels, as Sawston: in *Where Angels Fear to Tread* the town stands for narrowness, snobbery, unreality; in *The Longest Journey* the school is a deplorable institution. Forster had a lasting contempt for the public school and the public school attitude. In his essay *Notes on the English Character* he sees it at the root of grievous national faults. It sent people out into the world with 'well-developed bodies, fairly developed minds and undeveloped hearts', In *A Passage to India* he speaks of it 'flourishing [in India] more vigorously than it can hope to do in England' – brusquely dismissing the arts and religion, the English public school temperament, trained in restriction, in bottling up the emotions, chills and kills.

King's College, Cambridge, followed. In his biography of Goldsworthy Lowes Dickinson, he describes Dickinson's 'surprised relief to find that the public school is not infinite and eternal, that there is something more compelling in life than self-esteem and more vital than cricket, that firmness and self-complacency do not between them compose the whole armour of man.' This was a relief that Forster shared. It was indeed a different atmosphere: 'People and books re-inforced one another, intelligence joined hands with affection, speculation became a passion, and discussion was made profound by love'. The two became close friends, but the most powerful personal influence on Forster was that exerted by Nathaniel Wedd. In 1903 Wedd and Dickinson, together with G. M. Trevelyan, the historian, formed the *Independent Review*. It was, says Forster, who soon became a contributor, 'not so much a Liberal review as an appeal to Liberalism from the left to be its better self'.

Another powerful and related influence was that of what later came to be termed the Bloomsbury Group. In his autobiographical volume *Beginning Again* Leonard Woolf describes how most people comprising this close-knit group – amongst them Virginia Stephen (later Virginia Woolf), Maynard Keynes, Duncan Grant, Roger Fry, Desmond McCarthy, Forster and Woolf himself – had already been friends at Cambridge, members of the Conversation Society (the 'Apostles'), and had formed there a 'peculiar intimacy'. Woolf describes Forster as 'strange, elusive, evasive' and working underground like a mole to pop up every now and again with 'some subtle observation or delicate quip which somehow or other he had found in the depths of the earth or of his own soul'. But, however elusive or withdrawn from the central core of the group Forster was, the spirit of the times must certainly have entered into him. These intellectuals found themselves living 'in the spring-time of a conscious revolt' against established customs and beliefs. They felt, says Woolf, three profound passions: 'a passion for friendship, a passion for literature and music . . . a passion for what we called the truth'. It was, he says, 'tremendously exhilarating'. Forster shared this sense of exhilaration and experienced these passions.

In the years 1905–1910 his first four novels appeared. In 1912 he travelled to India in company with Dickinson and Trevelyan. During the war years he was on non-combatant duty in Egypt. He visisted India again in 1921. The record of these two visits is given in *The Hill of Devi*, 1953. One of their fruits was *A Passage to India*, published in 1924, the last of Forster's novels.

Besides his novels and other occasional pieces, Forster has written many short stories (most of which are contained in *The Celestial Omnibus*, 1914 and *The Eternal Moment*, 1928) a guide to Alexandria (published 1922), two full-scale biographies (*Goldsworthy Lowes Dickinson*, 1934 and *Marianne Thorton*, 1956). But his achievement rests on his five novels: *Where Angels Fear to Tread*, 1905; *The Longest Journey*, 1907; *A Room with a View*, 1908; *Howard's End*, 1910; *A Passage to India*, 1924. In these novels he pursues, with wit, intelligence and passion, his themes of the 'undeveloped heart', the struggle towards fullness of living and the supreme importance of 'the inner life'.

After Forster's death in 1970, another novel, *Maurice*, was published. It has a homosexual theme, and it seems unfinished, or at least unpolished. Before the First World War Forster also wrote many short stories. Most of these are fantastic or allegorical. They appear in *The Celestial Omnibus* (1911), and *The Eternal Moment* (1928).

In the second half of his life Forster was known chiefly as an essayist, critic and broadcaster. His essays appear in two collections, *Abinger Harvest* (1936) and *Two Cheers for Democracy* (1951). In 1927 he gave the Clark Lectures at Cambridge, which were published under the title of *Aspects of the Novel*. The last years of his life were spent in rooms at King's College, Cambridge.

Further reading

E. M. Forster, A Critical Study, Laurence Brander (Hart-Davis, MacGibbon)

E. M. Forster, The Personal Voice, John Colmer (Routledge & Kegan Paul)

The Writings of E. M. Forster, Rose Macaulay (Hogarth Press)

E. M. Forster, Lionel Trilling (Hogarth Press)

Background and plot

Background: a brief history of India and its religions

In about 2500 BC the flourishing urban Indus civilization emerged, to be destroyed about 1500 BC by Aryan invaders from the North-west, who drove the Dravidian inhabitants south and occupied the Ganges valley; they adopted Hinduism and introduced the caste system. In the sixth century BC the rival religions of Jains and Buddhists were introduced and exerted a dominating influence in the kingdom set up in 326 BC by Alexander the Great in the Punjab, and later ruled by Asoka. After conquest by the Huns and later the Arabs, a period of stability ensued. Subsequently Baber the Turk set up the Mogul Empire, with its capital at Delhi; the Great Moguls, of whom the most famous was Akbar, AD 1542–1605, were more powerful rulers than any before them.

With their decline, and the death of Auranzeb in 1707, came further invasions. Delhi was sacked by the Persians in 1739, while European intervention in India was growing. By the eighteenth century the British East India Company had set up posts at Madras, Bombay and Calcutta, the French at Pondicherry, and the Portuguese in Goa; after Clive's victory at Plassey in 1757, which gave control over Bengal, the British gradually eliminated French influence and brought the affairs of the company under the supervision of a Board. After the Indian Mutiny in 1857 India was taken under the full control of the British Government, though two-fifths of its area was still ruled by native princes. After 1880, the Indian nationalists demanded a share in political power; reforms in 1909, 1919 and 1935 were steps towards ultimate self-government, but too slow to satisfy them.

Hinduism

An ancient religion of India, Hinduism is based on the Vedas (holy writings in Sanskrit). It is a polytheistic religion, whose three principal gods, the *Trimurti* ('Triad') are: Brahma, the 'supreme god' (the Brahmins – highest Hindu caste – particularly worship Brahma); Vishnu, the 'preserver'; and Shiva, 'the destroyer'.

Islam

Like Christianity and Judaism, Islam is a monotheistic religion; it is based on the teachings of the prophet Mohammed (AD 570–632). The Koran is the Muslim holy book.

Geographical background

The map on p. 5 shows mainly the basin of the Ganges and the mountain ranges to the north and south. To the north are the Himalayas, and to the south the mountains of central India. These stretch right down the peninsula. They are 'older than anything in the world' and 'If flesh of the sun's flesh is to be touched anywhere, it is here, among the incredible antiquity of these hills' (Ch. 12). But the Ganges is encroaching on them, and they are 'sinking beneath the newer lands'. The 'Marabar Hills' of the novel are among the outposts which 'have been cut off and stand knee-deep, throat-deep, in the advancing soil'. 'Chandrapore' is on the Ganges, below Benares, 'edged rather than washed' by the river. It 'Trails for a couple of miles along the bank, scarcely distinguishable from the rubbish it deposits there' (Ch. 1). The 'Mau' of the novel is 'some hundreds of miles westward of the Marabar Hills' (Ch. 33). It is closely connected with the actual state of Dewas (see *The Hill of Devi*). Asirgarh is the town round which

Mrs Moore's train describes a semi-circle and which gives her the tantalizing and frustrating feeling that she has not seen the 'right places' (Ch. 23).

We are indebted to the late E. M. Forster for the following information: Chandrapore has 'some slight connection with Patna' and Mau is 'slightly connected with the town of the same name'. The Marabar Hills are based on the Barabar Hills south of Patna.

There is more than one Mau in India. The one marked on the map seems, perhaps, the one which has the 'slight connection' with the Mau of the book. (Fielding is on a 'tour through Central India' when he visits Godbole and Aziz there.) But there is a Mau on the Jumna west of Allahabad and another north of Allahabad; and, of course, as Forster's phrases indicate, precise identification is not to be sought.

Plot

The plot is, in its outline, conventional. Adela Quested has come out from England, with Mrs Moore, to Chandrapore. Her main motive is to see Ronny Heaslop, a Government official and Mrs Moore's son by her first marriage: she will move, it seems, smoothly towards engagement and marriage. But she wishes, too, to see the 'real India', to mingle with Indians socially, freely. At the house of Fielding, Principal of the Government College, she meets Dr Aziz. Between the Muslim doctor and the Englishman friendship is, precariously, beginning to grow. Aziz, impulsively, invites them – Adela, Mrs Moore, Fielding – to visit him at his home; but eventually withdraws this in favour of an outing to the Marabar Caves. Misfortune dogs the first stages of the outing; Mrs Moore, between whom and Aziz an instinctive bond of sympathy has quickly been sealed, is drained of vitality by her experience of the caves, with their hollow, echoing 'Boum'. She draws aside from further exploration and rests.

Adela suffers, it seems, some kind of hallucination (though everything is blurred), and leaves in distress. The English community eagerly seize on her confused accusations and she becomes convinced that Aziz has assaulted her sexually. Both Indians and English withdraw to rigidly defined racial positions. Fielding stands by Aziz, convinced of his innocence. Ronny persuades Mrs Moore, now querulous, detached, apparently lacking in sympathy with Adela, to go back to England. Aziz is brought to trial. At a critical moment in the prosecution's case Adela withdraws her accusation. In the confusion that follows Adela seeks social sanctuary in Government College, whilst the name of Mrs Moore, who has died on the voyage home, becomes a kind of talisman to the Indians – 'Esmiss Esmoor'. Adela's engagement to Ronny is broken – she has failed him and her country – and she departs for England. Fielding follows soon, on official business.

Time passes. Fielding marries Stella, Mrs Moore's daughter by her second marriage. Aziz meanwhile has become convinced that Fielding has married Adela (rumours had begun to spread immediately after the trial). Now bitterly anti-English, Aziz has withdrawn to a native court at Mau. Fielding returns to India and, with his wife and her brother Ralph, visits him there. In the presence of Ralph, Aziz feels the same chord of instinctive sympathy as Mrs Moore had struck. But, though the specific misunderstanding over the marriage is cleared up, deeper antipathies remain. Fielding and Aziz, less flexible individuals than they were at the time of their earlier crisis, less spontaneously generous, communicate over a gulf of racial discord. Personal friendship, relationship between individuals, is subject to the conditions of time and place. They cannot – not yet, not there – be friends.

Themes

The Imperial Theme

A Passage to India is much more than a novel about the political situation in India in the years following the 1914–18 war – and commentary on the novel must dwell on its more enduring character; but it certainly *is* a political novel which explores, with understanding and compassion, a political situation. It is now, perhaps, easy to be liberal and racially unprejudiced: it was certainly less easy at the time Forster wrote his novel. One should be aware of the intellectual courage with which Forster exposed the degrading effects of British rule. Notice how this theme of the novel emerges early, as, in Chapter 2, Hamidullah and Mahmoud Ali discuss 'whether or not it is possible to be friends with an Englishman'; and how it closes with the 'wrangle about politics' in which Fielding and Aziz engage – a 'wrangle' which certainly involves more than political conflict (two individuals are passionately involved, as people) but just as certainly does centre on the issue of Indian nationalism and the alien domination of England. In between the two can be seen the ingrained prejudice and obtuseness of Turton, the viciousness of Major Callendar and the complacency of Ronny. The Club, with its public school ethos, chokes the land. Alien rule imposes not simply political subjection but a distortion of natural normal ways of social intercourse, so that a small matter like an invitation to a party becomes a matter for worried discussion: and everyone – even Aziz in relation to Dr Panna Lal – breathes the 'prevalent miasma' of preoccupation with status and power. The novel is an attack on British rule.

The theme of 'place'

It is in this (traditional) manner that Forster's moral judgement operates. Ironical and explicit statement explores the actions of individuals as they pursue the daily round of social intercourse, existing amid a web of relationships that ranges from the passing to the intimate contact. Here is the part of the novel that the sparse words of the second chapter – 'whether or no it is possible to be friends with an Englishman' – adequately, in some degree, relate to.

But the novel moves in other ways, on other levels. This is clear in the first chapter, with its insistent stress on 'atmosphere', place, environment. Here is the city of Chandrapore: mean, squalid, ordinary – its few fine houses hidden away. The town, the inhabitants seem made of mud; and the organism that is the town persists in surviving ('swelling here, shrinking there') 'like some low but indestructible form of life'. But from the Civil Station the city seems an entirely different place – 'a tropical pleasaunce washed by a noble river'. The civil station itself 'provokes no emotion'. Above the ambiguous city and the dull civil station the sky arches itself (protectively or menacingly or neutrally?). And beyond that, beyond the stars, is that 'farther distance'.

It is the sky that 'settles everything'. It governs the earth, giving or withholding the rain. It acquires strength from the sun, and a sense of size from the 'prostrate earth'. The earth is indeed 'prostrate', for it stretches, league after league, with no mountain to 'infringe on the curve'. It is only to the south that the 'fist and fingers' of the Marabar Hills 'thrust up through the soil'. Here, in this intensely written paragraph, is an additional dimension of the novel: the sense of elusiveness (things are not only what they first appear to be; what *is* the truth?); the power of the elements – earth, rain and sky; the air of menace – as the hills which contain the 'extraordinary caves' thrust upwards.

The sense of oppression, unease, fear recurs at intervals throughout the novel; and usually associated with a sense of 'place'. After the inconclusive talk between Aziz and Fielding, Chapter 10 is full of a sense of foreboding. The heat had 'leapt forward'; humanity seems to have abandoned the city, the 'inarticulate world' to have taken over. The sun beats down, 'with power but without beauty'. This is sinister. And with all its brightness the sun was 'merely a creature like the rest, and so debarred from glory'.

In Chapter 12 Forster approaches the central horror of the Marabar Caves. ['When I began *A Passage to India* I knew that something important happened in the Marabar Caves and that it would have a central place in the novel – but I didn't know what it would be,' Forster has said in an interview with the *Paris Review*.] Here, too, is the note of menace; for the Marabar Hills are sinking beneath newer land, the plain of the Ganges is encroaching on them. So they stand as outposts of something ancient, mysterious; they rise 'abruptly, insanely, without the proportion that is kept by the wildest hills elsewhere'. Aziz's preparations for the outing meet many setbacks, for 'he had challenged the spirit of the Indian earth, which tries to keep men in compartments'. The earth is inimical to human intermingling. The hills rearing violently upwards are a sign of this.

Within the hills are the Marabar Caves; and within the caves is the destructive echo, which so confounds both Adela and Mrs Moore. Here, Mrs Moore feels, has spoken 'something snub-nosed, incapable of generosity – the underlying worm itself'. It exists here, in this place – though its power spreads, echo-like. As Mrs Moore leaves India, in 'the soupy dawn of Bombay', she feels that India, the place, has defeated her: she has not 'seen the right places'. As she leaves the palm-trees mock her.

Chapter 33 describes Fielding's journey home: and here again places echo or symbolize his feelings. Alexandria is bright and clear, contrasting with the 'intricacies of Bombay'; Crete seems to welcome him; and in Venice, in St Mark's, he finds 'the harmony between the works of man and the earth that upholds them, the civilization that has escaped muddle, the spirit in a reasonable form, with flesh and blood subsisting'. Indeed, the Mediterranean, he feels, is 'the human norm'; away from that, one approaches the 'monstrous and the extraordinary'. And 'tender romantic fancies' flowered in Fielding's mind as he saw the English countryside. Here is a 'place, a landscape, an earth that is not hostile to human desires.

'Muddle'

An atmosphere of frustration, 'muddle', pervades everything. This is a fact of life (Mrs Moore had learnt, as Adela had not, that 'adventures do occur, but not punctually'); but it is especially a fact of life in India. The first indications in the novel are apparently trivial events. Ronny is mistaken over the identity of 'the doctor' whom Mrs Moore has met. Thinking the doctor is a European he had 'brought out all the comradely emotions', only to retire in irritation when he realizes that it is Aziz. 'What a mix-up!' There is confusion, 'misunderstanding', over the carriage of the Bhattacharyas, which never turns up. The dialogue between Adela, Mrs Moore and Fielding over 'mystery and muddle' follows. Mrs Moore likes mysteries but not muddles: Fielding tells her that one is a high-sounding term for the other and that he and Aziz know that India is a muddle.

The whole incident of the Marabar Caves is suffused with muddle. The dawn promises to be a 'miracle' but 'at the supreme moment' everything misfires – nothing occurs. Adela and Mrs Moore long for the tidy, manageable romance of Grasmere. It is never clear what actually happens in the cave: this, too, is a muddle, a mystery – the central, reverberating fact, never clarified, of the whole novel. When Fielding finally commits himself to the Indian side in the battle, he foresees that besides tragedy there will be muddle, as he insists that native troops are much better than English for this country. Fielding's gesture of commitment to the Indian side is no striking, lucid action but a refusal to stand when Ronny enters the club: not a wholly satisfying gesture – his quarrel was not specifically with Ronny, and he had some sympathy for him – but 'there it was, done, muddled through'. The dessication of the spirit that Mrs Moore suffers at the time of Aziz's trial is described as 'a spiritual muddledom', in which neither the claim of this world nor the claim of the next speaks with a clear voice: 'we can neither act nor refrain from action, we can neither ignore nor respect infinity'. Her name becomes a kind of charm to the Indians – in the garbled form of 'Esmiss Esmoor'.

The court scene ends in confusion, just as Adela's retraction has broken through the clouds of her confused mind. Confusion attends the festivities afterwards, as Fielding and Adela are deposited in the grounds of the Government College; and conflicting expectations (the Indians wishing to press home claims for compensation, Fielding urging compassion) mar, to some degree, the moment of triumph. Aziz, at first partly and then wholly, believes the rumours that Fielding has had an affair with Adela. Confusion flourishes and he leaps, eagerly, to the conclusion that the marriage is to Adela. As Fielding travels home he reaches Venice and his heart goes out to St Mark's, the symbol of 'the civilization that escaped muddle'.

In Chapter 33 'muddle' has a different significance. The ceremony is jumbled, ragged and confused; the 'approaching triumph of India was a muddle (as we call it), a frustration of reason and Form'. Hindu music and 'Nights of Gladness' mingle; Professor Godbole's pince-nez, having caught in a jasmine garland, 'lay sideways on his nose'; the god is born and yet not born; the Rajah is dead but his death is concealed; butter spreads around in a divine mess. Here, in fact, Forster celebrates *with* Godbole, it seems, as he 'develops the life of the spirit'. The ceremony evokes a spiritual serenity, beyond its muddle, that the West cannot achieve.

But the dominating impression left by the sense of muddle, the many incidents involving confusion, misunderstanding and doubt, is one of frustration, the baffling of human endeavour, the futility of the human desire for certainty and solid achievement.

The Echo and Evil

In this atmosphere, in this place, in these circumstances (of alien domination), evil flourishes. The most potent symbol in the book – in which there are many symbols, stating, re-inforcing Forster's meaning – is that of the echo. Its power reverberates from the cave, the 'source', as it were, of the novel. But before we hear of the echo in the caves the word has occurred in contexts that prepare the reader for its full impact and relate the impression of the spiritual evil generated in the cave, to the more human 'earthy' evil that exists in society. At the Bridge Party Adela is frustrated in her desire to make contact with 'friendly Indians': she is met by the 'echoing walls of their civility'. Meditating after an unsatisfactory conversation with Ronny, Mrs Moore finds herself more preoccupied with the name of 'God' than usual and yet she has never found the uttering of his name less efficacious than she does now: 'Outside the arch there seemed always an arch, beyond the remotest echo a silence'.

Aziz dwells nostalgically on the memory of his wife, evoked by the photograph from which she looks out, in bewilderment, at the 'echoing contradictory world'. Then, in the Marabar caves, Mrs Moore meets the 'terrifying echo'. It is an echo that, unlike the many 'exquisite echoes' of India, is 'devoid of distinction', a hollow boum, boum, boum that reduces all human endeavour to nothing: 'everything exists and nothing has value.'' After her experience there Mrs Moore feels that her hold on life is undermined. She is 'terrified over an area larger than usual' and loses all desire to communicate with anyone. She sits 'motionless with horror'.

The echo has alarmed Adela, too. She had struck the polished wall just before the incident, the 'assault'. The echo of that action lives in her disordered mind as a token of the evil that has been let loose. She seeks Mrs Moore but she will not come and so 'the echo flourished'. The noise in the cave, so insignificant in itself, 'was prolonged over the surface of her life'. It is a symbol of the intellectual blindness that accompanies Adela's distraught state. Mrs Moore tells her that she will never get rid of the echo. But when she feels for a moment that she has made a mistake it goes away – 'My echo's better'. It returns at the trial when she is determined to support those who are pursuing the charge. After the trial and her recantation it disappears again.

But as Mrs Moore leaves India, realizing she has not seen the 'right places', the palm trees seem to mock her: 'So you thought an echo was India; you took the Marabar caves as final?'. (They were not 'final'; but India keeps her secret, inaccessible to the European mind – and it is as a European, defeated, that Mrs Moore leaves India, sent packing by her son.)

The echo is present first in isolated metaphorical phrase, then as literal fact (the caves *do* echo), then ultimately, woven into the realistic texture of the novel through the powerful evocation of the Marabar Caves, it takes on, easily, the significance of symbol. It is a fitting symbol.

There is something haunting, ominous about an echo. Released by a specific sound, it then seems to gather and acquire a life of its own; there is, too, an elusiveness about it, a kind of mystery. Here, then, is the fact of evil that exists in the novel; released by human action, on the uncongenial soil of India, aided by the confusion and muddle that attends human endeavour there, it flourishes, spreads, mocking human efforts to subdue it.

Hallucination

In this world people move in a muffled dream. Part of the strange power of the book, part of its distinctive vision, in fact, is this sense of human beings moving, in frustration, certainly, but also in a trance-like manner, through experiences that have a life and compulsion of their own. This life is often menacing, evil. Chandrapore shrinks and swells 'like some low but indestructible form of life'. The Marabar Hills are like grotesque 'fists and fingers' and, menacingly, they thrust upwards. As Mrs Moore looks lovingly at the small wasp, outside the baying of the jackals mingles with the percussion of the drums and her voice 'floated out, to swell the night's uneasiness'. The hot weather is felt as a hostile presence. It is a vague threat, and the sun beats down 'with power but without beauty'. The source of everything seems to be in the Marabar Hills. The experience the traveller has of them is elusive; perhaps one has had no experience at all. Language cannot describe them.

Aziz and his party travel to this 'experience', to these caves, on the outing that no one really wanted, amidst scenery that echoes their desultory frame of mind: 'The scene was agreeable rather than not in the mild morning air, but there was little colour in it, and no vitality.' Pervading everything is the sense of dream, hallucination, menace. A kind of 'spiritual silence' invades 'more senses than the ear'; and this silence seems unhealthy, sick: 'Everything seemed cut off at its root, and therefore infected with illusion.' Confusion grows. What are the mounds? The black cobra turns out to be a withered stump. Heat radiates and creates its own distorted images. As they enter the caves they are 'sucked in like water down a drain'. The earth has a prehistoric air, seeming alien to man. Their reappearance is described thus: 'And then the hole belched and humanity returned.' The word 'belched' is powerfully suggestive. It conveys the feeling that the cave has a power and will of its own, that it rejects in distaste the human beings who visit it, and that there is disorder, sickness there.

The whole party have moved, through scenery that seems to share and re-inforce their apathy, to an experience which deprives them even more completely of their will power. Mrs Moore drifts henceforth on waves of indifference, disgust, irritation, spiritual ennui. Adela suffers the pain of continually re-living an experience of which the only thing she is sure is that it was shameful and disruptive. Aziz is directly and painfully affected, on the 'surface' of his life at first, but then more deeply. He becomes harder, eventually bitter.

In the court the air of hallucination recurs in its full power. Adela does not will herself to 'remember' in any normal sense of the word but she 'returned to the Marabar Hills, and spoke from them across a sort of darkness.' Here is an utter surrender of will. The day takes on 'the indescribable splendour' of a vision. She listens, in a trance, to the voice of Macbride, leading her, like some priest, 'along the paths of truth'. She is wafted on, dream-like, by the airs of the punkah, pulled by the man of god-like splendour. The court awaits in silence her reply to the question (which is hardly a question), 'And the prisoner followed you.' But Adela could not reply 'until Aziz entered the place of answer'. Note the form of Forster's statement here. Adela is waiting for the next fact of her re-created experience to occur. She is waiting for the incident that will release, as it were, her next words. She is passive, wafted on, and now rendered silent – for Aziz will not enter 'the place of answer'. Her final withdrawal of the charge is given, when it comes, in 'hard, prosaic tones'. She has returned to the 'insipidity of the world', her vision is over. Life, too, returns to its normal complexities. Only the 'beautiful naked god' continues, in his trance of ignorance and detachment, to pull the cord of his punkah and to gaze at the scene before him.

The novel then stays, mainly, in the 'insipid world'. Human beings struggle, against their own imperfection and against the oppressive presence of the Indian earth which falls 'like a gravestone on any human hope'. But a large part, and a significant part, of the novel has been suffused with this atmosphere of illusion, trance, unwilled drifting towards a disastrous end. In this respect it has the air, if not of nightmare, then of a troubled dream.

Personal relationships

The theme of personal relationships could be said to be the important one in all of Forster's novels. *Howard's End*, the novel in which he states most explicitly the things that deeply concern him, centres on the conflict between two families and two ways of living. The Wilcoxes represent the 'outer life', the life in which 'telegrams and anger' count; the Schlegels represent the 'inner life', in which personal relationships are supreme. Here, indeed, is the subject of *A Passage to India* too. Placed in the India of the second decade of this century and closely involved with the political implications of the situation of that time, which it explores with a courageous topical relevance, the novel, nevertheless, transcends political and local conditions. Forster depicts people moving, in the adverse conditions of human situations, towards a full development of themselves, and, consequent on this, a full and living relationship with other people. People move *towards* this; they do not always achieve it. One may look at three particular incidents in the novel – one centrally important, the other two rather on the fringes – and feel the intense sympathy with which Forster sees people involved with each other in this way.

In Chapter 26 Fielding and Hamidullah mention the death of Mrs Moore. Fielding speaks of the growth of the legends surrounding her name. Hamidullah 'smiled, and looked at his watch'. His near-indifference is shared by Fielding, for they were 'middle-aged men, who had invested their emotions elsewhere'. Forster comments that it is only 'one's own dead who matter' – one cannot be sorry for all the sadness that meets one on the face of the earth. He adds that 'the soul is tired in a moment', and, 'fearing to lose the little she does understand', retreats and suffers in the ways that habit or chance has dictated. There is no indifference here on Forster's part, but compassion for those who have the capacity to suffer. The capacity, though, is finite. Fielding has expended his; Hamidullah is detached anyway. It is a mark of the quality of Forster's insight that he can feel for the fatigue as well as for the intensity of the human soul.

A moving paragraph describes the parting of Fielding and Adela – an Adela who has been changed by her experience. They are both 'at the height of their powers' – controlled sophisticated, intelligent Europeans – and there is complete communication between them. Yet they both feel dissatisfied. They do not think they are wrong, as they assert that they wish to go on living or that they do not believe in God, but a 'wistfulness' descends on them and 'the shadow of the shadow of a dream fell over their clear-cut interests, and objects never seen again seemed like messages from another world'.

Finally the novel moves to its piercing climax. As Aziz and Fielding take their last ride together, their 'last free intercourse', the scenery '[falls] like a gravestone on any human hope'. In the good, hard impersonal wrangle about politics they move, ironically, towards their moment of deepest intimacy. Aziz's tirade against English imperialism culminates poignantly, as he rides furiously against Fielding, 'half kissing him', in a vision of the day when, 'every blasted Englishman' driven into the sea, he and Fielding can be friends. Fielding pleads for that friendship now: 'It's what I want. It's what you want.' But as they move together in love, their love is denied. The horses swerve apart, moving in single file through the sundering rocks; the hundred voices of India call out, 'No, not yet'; and the over arching sky calls out, 'No, not there'.

Style

Forster's style is not distinctively unusual. By the time *A Passage to India* was published several writers, seeking to express their own unique vision, had found the traditional patterns of the English language inadequate to their purposes. James Joyce (1882—1941) had wrestled violently with conventional syntax and even with the existing vocabulary. In his *Ulysses*, written between 1914 and 1921, sentences take strange forms: in one section of the book compressed and elliptical; in another flowing, without punctuation, from page to page; in another imitating, or parodying, rhythms and forms that other writers have used with skill. In his *The Rainbow*, published in 1915, D. H. Lawrence (1885—1930) had sought at times a fluid relaxed manner that would penetrate with ease those hidden paths of the human mind that he wished to explore. Virginia Woolf (1882—1941) had moved towards a formal arrangement and patterning, with the quick shifts of thought and mood conveyed obliquely in deftly formulated phrases.

Forster was, it seems, untouched by these experiments. One thinks of Jane Austen (1775—1817). Forster's prose is in the manner, in the tradition that she brought to complete definition at the end of the eighteenth century. It has lost the air of formal balance but has kept the precise clarity.

Precision and clarity

Precision and clarity are general terms, and do not mean much without exact illustration. The last paragraph of the first chapter provides rich proof. The first statement is lucid, dogmatic in its straightforwardness: 'The sky settles everything.' This statement seems to hold out little promise of further enlightenment. However the sky settles 'not only climates and season' but 'when the earth shall be beautiful'. The sentence moves, with charm and power, to this conclusion. It is a conclusion that is very significant, for the sky is an (equivocal) emblem of hope in the novel and here it gives a blessing to the earth, the blessing of beauty. The whole sentence moves, with ease, towards this statement. The next sentence, brief again, dismisses the earth quickly. Then, in the sentence beginning 'But when the sky chooses,' the prose moves with a graceful power. The sharpness of power, of the sentence and of the sky, is in the verb 'rain' and the sweep of power in the final phrase, 'or a benediction pass from horizon to horizon'. The next sentence has a casual strength: 'The sky can do this because it is so strong and so enormous.' Then the prose is clipped, compressed: 'Strength comes from the sun, infused in it daily, size from the prostrate earth.' The omission of the verb 'comes' after 'size' has much to do with the effect.

'No mountains infringe on the curve' states, concisely, a new idea. 'Infringe' gives a sense of the dominating sweep of the sky that no mountain dare meddle with. The next sentence has a three fold structure: three verbs ('lies flat', 'heaves', 'is flat') conveying the insistent sweep of the land to the horizon. Now, without haste, comes the qualification. The novel will reveal the hills as sinister. They do not give a blessing as the sky does. The note of menace is caught in the word 'thrust'. Here is something powerful and unusual (for it breaks the sweep of the land). In the last sentence 'fists and fingers' hint at some kind of human will. There is something uncanny about these human shapes that intrude on the flat plain. The paragraph ends with the bare statement that these are 'the Marabar Hills, containing the extraordinary caves'. The word 'extraordinary' acts in three ways. It takes one back to the first sentence of the book, and alerts one to the probable significance of the caves in the unfolding of the novel. It is in harmony with the tone of quiet, undramatic statement that colours the whole chapter. It carries (in retrospect perhaps, as one holds it in one's mind and remembers it instinctively as the novel progresses), a note of disquiet – something is not as it should be.

The paragraph has the virtues of precision and clarity. But it is precision and clarity that says a great deal. There is no dullness of statement, but a lucid prose that makes its lucid statements and also carries implications of meaning. It works at more than one level, and it seeks for a deep and thoughtful response from the reader.

Metaphor and simile

Metaphor and simile are indispensable, but Forster uses them with discretion. His prose is not highly figurative, but when they come the figures of speech are striking. The town swells and shrinks 'like some low but indestructible form of life'. The stars 'hang like lamps from the immense vault' of the sky. The Marabar Hills we have seen thrusting themselves up like 'fists and fingers'. Aziz feels 'caught in the meshes' of the civil station. The sense of harmony with the universe that Mrs Moore feels as she looks at the moon 'passed into the old woman and out, like water through a tank, leaving a strange freshness behind'.

European dress had 'lighted like a leprosy' on the Indians who attended the Bridge Party. In their nervousness three of the Indian women 'suddenly shot out of the summerhouse like exquisitely coloured swallows' – graceful, elegant, elusive and nervous. A conversation between Adela, Aziz and Mrs Moore is broken by an error of Adela's and it lay 'scattered like the petals of a desert flower'. This contact was a frail growth. Beautiful but frail. The place from which all the caves seem to originate is 'their original spawning place'. Here is the suggestion of the low mean life that is hinted at in the first paragraph of the novel.

wind fall out of the sky and then 'bounce back into it'. The train taking the party on the Marabar outing 'wobbled away through the fields'. A patch of field jumps 'as though it is being fried'. Aziz' eyes are like 'black bullets'. A punkah flaps 'dirty petticoats' over Fielding's and Turton's heads at the waiting room.

That which exists in the caves is something 'snub-nosed'. The abyss may be 'petty', the 'serpent of eternity made of maggots'. In the turmoil and heat that follows Aziz's release it seems as if 'the heat of the sun had boiled and fried all the glories of the earth into a single mess.' The relationship between Adela and Fielding 'petered out'. As Adela left Bombay the sea 'slid like broth against the quays'. As Fielding leaves Chandrapore 'the heaven and earth both looked like toffee'. Here is a readiness to use the sinewy elemental words. The novel is no frail delicate thing unable to stand the intrusion of the earthy. It is profound, sensitive *and* earthy – and the hard, harsh words that punctuate its progress are a sign of this.

Dialogue

It is quickly apparent what a large part dialogue plays in the novel. One sign of Forster's skill here is the way in which he catches the idiom of different characters. The Eurasian chauffeur, caught between two worlds, speaks in a manner that echoes his position in no-man's-land: 'You give me five minutes' time, I'll take you any dam anywhere'; 'By Jove, sir, your lady is right', 'Half a moment. Give me ten minutes' time.' Miss Derek, 'all friskiness and friendliness', produces the exclamations one expects – 'But how putrid!', 'How absolutely rotten!' – and the genteel exaggeration that aims to turn all life into a ludicrous game: 'The whole of India seethes with Mahranis and Ranis and Begums who clamour for such as me.' Adela, more naïvely, exhibits her essential lack of feeling: 'I want to see the real India', 'A Mahomeddan, how perfectly magnificent', 'Mrs Moore, may I put our difficulty to Dr Aziz, I mean our Anglo-Indian one?'

The Anglo-Indian mentality is trapped in recurring phrases: 'Did you gather he was well disposed?'; 'It's the educated native's latest dodge'; 'You can't run with the hare and hunt with the hounds, at least not in this country'; 'Have a peg'. Consider how the excitability and incipient tenderness of Aziz is caught in his words to Mrs Moore, at their first meeting: 'Mrs Moore, this is all extremely strange, because like yourself I have also two sons and a daughter. Is not this the same box with a vengeance?' And, later, 'You understand me, you know what others feel. Oh, if others resembled you!' The same delicate, slightly incorrect, idiom is caught again, when he says to Ralph Moore, 'Perhaps I will just take you out on the water now, for one short half-hour.'

These are people who are either seeking to express themselves in an idiom that is not their native one, or whose language has taken the same rigid and distinctive forms as their unnatural way of life. Forster conveys finely the oddity, the pressure of alien circumstances.

The same kind of perception and control is evident in the progress of dialogue between two characters. Notice the edgy conversation between Fielding and Macbride in Chapter 18. At the beginning somewhere near making contact, they gradually diverge as their basic attitudes are revealed to each other, and the conflict becomes explicit in this dramatic interchange:

'But *I* wanted to ask her. I want someone who believes in him to ask her.'
'What difference does that make?'
'She is among people who disbelieve in Indians.'
'Well, she tells her own story, doesn't she?'
'I know, but she tells it to you.'

See too, how Fielding's frustration with Godbole's lack of

directness, as the Englishman seeks a straight answer, is conveyed in 'A name? A name for a school?' and in the weary, appealing, 'Godbole!' which follows the Hindu's careful explanation that he does not expect an immediate answer to his question.

The dialogue between Aziz and Fielding at the beginning of Chapter 27 (p. 250) catches beautifully the tone of lazy intimacy, relaxed delight in triumph that both men are feeling. Few writers have conveyed so precisely the atmosphere of that kind of moment:

'. . . I have become anti-British, and ought to have done so sooner, it would have saved me numerous misfortunes.'
'Including knowing me.'
'I say, shall we go and pour water onto Mohammed Latif's face? He is so funny when this is done to him asleep.'

The novel is full of such perceived and finely created moments of insight. The unobtrusive style expresses with exactitude the thought, feeling and invention that compose the whole.

Symbols

Forster's style also includes the use of symbols to convey the complex aspects of his vision. These symbols are not merely counters used to convey meanings which plot and situation cannot themselves indicate but are closely woven into the texture of the whole novel, convincing both in their literal meanings and in their more powerful evocations.

The *'echo'* theme has already been discussed. It is also a symbol associated with frustration, error, mistaken interpretations and evil. Once released by action – the attempt to make contact at an intimate level – the echo flourishes and grows. Human effort cannot restrain it. Closely linked with the echo is another symbol, the cave. The incident in the caves is the central one of the whole novel, indeed its starting point in Forster's mind. It is in the cave that the echo occurs. The caves are dark and mysterious – a fitting place for misfortune. It is this that they symbolize.

Fire is another symbol: within the mosque the flame of friendship between Aziz and Mrs Moore is kindled. Under its influence Aziz certainly feels intensely the fact that he is a Moslem (the power of Islam, which is 'his own country, more than a Faith, more than a battle-cry, more, much more'); but this brings to him not a feeling of hostility but of unity, harmony. And when Mrs Moore feels her sudden sense of kinship with the heavenly bodies the mosque is nearby, gleaming into sight.

The *'flame'* of friendship which springs up in the mosque does not spread its power. The 'fire of good fellowship' that is kindled between Aziz and the subaltern as they play at polo soon cools, as their bodies cool (for athletics can rouse only a 'temporary glow'); and in the cave, as the visitor strikes a match, the two flames – that of the match and that of its reflection in the smoothly polished walls – 'strive to unite' but fail, for 'one of them breathes air, the other stone'. Here is an emblem of the striving to unite that is the central theme of the novel.

Perhaps the linked symbolism of *arch and sky* penetrates most nearly to the heart of the novel. In the first chapter the sky is an 'overarching sky'. At the Bridge Party 'impartial' kites hover overhead in a sky that is also impartial; and the sequence seems infinite: 'beyond the sky must not there be something that overarches all the skies, more impartial even than they. Beyond which again . . . ' The thought fades – and one returns to *Cousin Kate*. Mrs Moore's troubled mind is described thus: 'Outside the arch there seemed always an arch, beyond the remotest echo a silence'. As Ronny and Adela make spurious contact in the Nawab Bahadur's car the night sky encircles them, seeming absolute but in fact itself only a 'spurious unity', for it is 'modified by the gleams of day that leaked up round the edges of the world, and by the stars'. On the Marabar Caves outing the dawn is an anti-climax. After the trial, when unreason and hatred seem to be spreading, Fielding sees the 'fists and fingers' of the Marabar Hills swelling 'until they include the whole night sky'. At the close it is the sky which gives the equivocal response to Fielding's plea for friendship now – 'No, not yet'. So the sky is an enclosing arch, enfolding everything beneath it in a unity, but a unity that is deceptive, 'spurious'. There is no unity, no certainty: and the sky with its sense of infinitely receding horizons, its spaces into which echoes spread and linger, becomes the embodiment of the vagueness of everything, the elusiveness, the absence of anything final, precise, exact. Certainty fades in this place, on this earth, beneath this sky: beyond the arch, which seems to offer a final resting place, there is no secure abode but always another arch. The mind is baffled and frustrated in the search.

Satire

The satire that runs through many scenes makes no unexpected claims on a reader whose expectations of what a novel is have been set by the tradition that runs from Fielding, Fanny Burney, through Jane Austen to modern times. The note, it seems, is often of wry detachment; the atmosphere rarely becomes acrid. The Bridge Party is sad but comic. European costume had 'lighted like a leprosy . . . Few had yielded entirely, but none were untouched.' A small group of Indian women gathers near the summer house, 'in which the more timid of them had taken refuge'; others stand with their backs to the company 'and their faces pressed into a bank of shrubs'. The note is one of a sophisticated, unalarmed amusement. The ludicrous aloofness of Mrs Turton, disdain sharpened into anxiety as she realizes that some of the Indian women are Westernized and can judge her by her own standards, is exactly caught as she admits that they may have passed Paris on their way to London – 'as if she was describing the movement of migratory birds'.

The phrase, too, sparks off another one: as Adela and Mrs Moore leave 'three ladies who had hitherto taken no part in the reception suddenly shot out of the summer house like exquisitely coloured swallows, and salaamed them'. Indeed the ironic light that plays upon the Indians so frequently is an affectionate one. The poor relation of Hamidullah's, only 'slightly immersed in the realms of matter', succeeds, with the aid of a servant, in guiding the bicycle over a tin-tack. Despite his protestations, Aziz does, in fact, 'dally to clean his teeth'. Dr Pannal Lal shakes the thermometer down, 'so that its altitude remained for ever unknown'. Professor Godbole's hand encounters food 'as it were by stealth'; and his conversation frequently 'culminated in a cow'.

Distaste sharpening into detestation controls Forster's picture of the English community. Macbride, with his theory of climatic zones, is seen with some sympathetic amusement, but the rest is gritty dislike. The 'Hear, hear!' which places the matter of Heaslop being a sahib 'beyond all doubt'; Turton's inventive 'Bridge Party', a phrase that 'amuses all who hear it'; the pregnant implications of 'well-disposed'; the National Anthem, which stiffens the will; the eager proclamation of indifference to the arts and the gruff dismissal of religion; *Cousin Kate* . . . these are the minutiae of a world from which Forster recoils. He understands clearly the working of group emotionalism:

For a few hours an exalted emotion gushed forth, which the women felt even more keenly than the men, if not for so long. 'What can we do for our sister?' was the only thought of Mesdames Callendar and Lesley, as they drove through the pelting heat to enquire.

They exchanged the usual drinks but everything tasted

different and then they looked out at the palisade of cactuses stabbing the purple throat of the sky; they realised they were thousands of miles from any scenery that they understood.

They had started speaking of 'women and children' – the phrase that exempts the male from sanity when it has been repeated a few times.

Forster senses, too 'the staleness and ungenerosity', the lack of true affection and concern. Early in the novel Ronny asserts, with sincerity, that the English are not in India to be pleasant; and Mrs Moore listens:

His words without his voice might have impressed her, but when she saw the self-satisfied lilt of them, when she saw the mouth moving so complacently and competently beneath the little red nose, she felt, quite illogically, that this was not the last word on India.

What Ronny lacks, and it is a characteristic lack, is 'one touch of regret – not the canny substitute but the true regret from the heart'.

As Fielding and Adela say farewell to each other 'a friendliness, as of dwarfs shaking hands, was in the air'. The simile portrays poignantly the haunting elusiveness of this moment. Godbole's festival is a 'great blur'. No man could say where the 'emotional centre' of it was, 'any more than he could locate the heart of a cloud'. As Fielding and Aziz take their last ride together the scenery, 'though it smiled, fell like a gravestone on any human hope'. The death of their intimacy is near; the Indian earth is triumphant.

These are only a few instances of the figurative power of Forster's language. Notice that metaphor and simile are not used as decorations but are means towards a full, complete statement. The statement is not complete without the image (i.e. the metaphor or simile). One should note, too, Forster's use of symbols. These are metaphors that pervade the book. They are used with a consistency of meaning and they carry much of the weight of deeper meaning in the novel. (The section on symbols speaks of this aspect of Forster's style.)

Vocabulary

The vocabulary of *A Passage to India* is, of course, that of a highly civilized and refined mind. There is no seeking for the out-of-the-way word for its own sake, but Forster uses the full resources of the language. A good dictionary will be an essential aid to the student. He will have to use it only occasionally, but he will certainly have to use it. The novelist does not, however, ignore the simpler everyday words. Indeed one distinctive mark of his style in this novel is the quite frequent use of the spiky colloquial word or phrase. There is nothing rarefied about Forster's art. So the hookah 'bubbles sulkily'. Aziz 'whizzed' out of Hamidullah's compound. The Government College had been 'slapped down' by the Public Works Department. Blasts of

Characters

Aziz

His life though vivid was largely a dream.

Early in their relationship Aziz misunderstands a remark of Fielding's – about Post-Impressionism – and withdraws into a momentary stiffness. This vanishes almost immediately for, Forster says, the Indian felt the Englishman's fundamental good-will and his own good-will went out to meet it. Forster then adds that Aziz was sensitive rather than responsive, that in every remark he found a meaning, but not always the correct one and that 'his life though vivid was largely a dream.' Much of the essence of Aziz is contained here: a person swayed by currents of emotion, instincts; acting as his temperament, his nature demands; seeking and finding significance in the passing remark even; and living at that heightened level of sensitivity that one often experiences in dreams. There is much more to him than this; but perhaps here is 'the essential life'.

One sees him first animatedly greeting Hamidullah. He talks and chaffs with zest. There is in him, and in the whole company, that 'fundamental gaiety' that bubbles up when they are with their own people. He feels oppressed by the dullness, the rigidity of the Civil Station and English ways – 'everything ranged coldly on shelves'. The poetic themes he prefers are 'the decay of Islam and the brevity of love'. Indeed he always considers pathos to be profound! He indulges in self-pity as he gazes at the photograph of his dead wife; but genuine emotion soon mingles with this. She had indeed been a unique experience for him; and the only name for that experience was 'love'. He wonders whether he will meet her in an after-life, and, characteristically, his opinion fluctuates, 'the corpuscles of his blood' rather than any effort of the reasoning mind seeming to determine which opinion he should hold at any particular time.

He understands Godbole's reticence about the Marabar Caves, for he himself 'suffered from similar inhibitions'. With Major Callendar, and to his exasperation, he would, sometimes, pass over the one relevant fact in a situation to dwell on irrelevant ones. Here again his mind, his reason, was in abeyance, subdued on these occasions not by 'the corpuscles of the blood' but by some other power that he was unable to control.

On the social level he is moved by impulses: to offer Fielding his collar-stud; to invite Adela and Mrs Moore to his (untidy) bungalow; to escape from this into the ambitious invitation to them all to 'see [him] in the Marabar Caves'. When the 'secure and intimate note' of Fielding's tea-party is jarred into disharmony by Ronny's brusque intrusion, Aziz is himself jarred into a discordant extravagance of manner. Again, at the mercy of a mood he becomes 'greasily confidential' to Adela, 'loud and jolly' towards Godbole. Later shocked by Adela's tactless inquiries he plunges into one of the caves to recover his composure. His sensitiveness on this point – her remark had been unworthy of a guest, he feels – leads him to be inaccurate over the details of what had actually happened when he and Adela parted. Here a kind of sensitive delicacy, irrational, instinctive, leads to his downfall.

Aziz responds instinctively, generously to kindness, sympathy, love. His heart goes out fully to Mrs Moore. He feels in her the kind of intuitive understanding that he has longed for. She is no European but a Moslem! This affection survives without a tremor. When, much later, he meets Ralph Moore it wells up again in his heart. It is, he realizes, illogical: Mrs Moore did not speak in his defence or even visit him in prison. Yet she had 'stolen to the depths of his heart,' and now, (his heart 'too full to draw back' from the feared cycle of friendship followed by disaster), he takes

Ralph out on the lake, an act of homage to his mother.

Imprisonment has changed Aziz to some extent. It has made 'channels for his character, which would never fluctuate as widely now as in the past'. He has become 'harder and less approachable', sternly anti-English – 'they had even thrown nets over his dreams' of an Indian motherland. His retreat to Mau was based on impulse – a 'sound' impulse, says Forster. There his temperament, once channelled in European ways, runs free again and 'he let his instruments rust, ran his little hospital at half-steam, and caused no undue alarm' (a Moslem at a Hindu court).

His friendship with Fielding survives this change, but not without difficulty. The Englishman's persistence on Adela's behalf frustrates Aziz's idyllic dream of a holiday together in Kashmir or Persia, subsidised by the damages obtained from Adela. In Aziz's mind belief and disbelief could exist together and, as he had 'no sense of evidence', 'the sequence of his emotions' governs what he believes at any particular time. He believes the rumours about Adela and Fielding. Rancour grows in his mind in Fielding's absence. He no longer wishes to meet him. Fielding's letter, incompletely read by Aziz, confirms his suspicions. When they do meet again, it is in gritty discord. And, when the misunderstanding over Fielding's wedding is cleared up, Aziz, dominated by emotions of shame and rage, clings to the life that he has built on a mistake. The 'irrefragable logic' of Fielding makes no impression on this fabric that Aziz has constructed: 'I wish no Englishman to be my friend'.

The collision on the lake works a kind of benign magic. Emotions of national hatred and personal love mingle in Aziz as the novel moves to its climax.

He is drawn with tender, firm affection.

Fielding

The world, he believed, is a globe of men who are trying to reach one another and do so by the help of good will plus culture and intelligence.

The character of Fielding does not impress the English reader so freshly, with such an impact of novelty as does that of Aziz. One is familiar with the qualities and defects of such a man as Fielding; whereas one has, in a sense, to take Forster's Aziz on trust. (The truth of the character emerges through one's convictions of the power of the art.) One's familiarity with such a 'stock type' as the well-meaning liberal is not, in fact, a help to an appreciation of Forster's skill. Preconceptions of what such a character should be may blind us to what he actually *is*. Fielding is not, indeed, a stock type, but is drawn with delicate insight and technical skill.

Fielding came to India comparatively late in his life. He was neither a young man seeing India for the first time nor a seasoned Anglo-Indian returning. He received, of course, new impressions but they were not the orthodox ones. Conditioned by his past, he had a tendency to see India as Italy and the Indians as Italians (both countries were peninsulas!). He has had a varied scholastic career and has succeeded with his pupils at the Government College at Chandrapore. But he has felt a gulf widening between himself and his fellow-countrymen. Their distrust of him is well-founded, for he believes in ideas and ideas disruptive in the Indian situation. Moreover he 'used ideas by that most potent method – interchange'. He believes, naïvely, that different peoples are striving to connect with each other and can do so with the help of 'goodwill plus culture and intelligence'. He has developed in an environment in which racial prejudice cannot flourish. He has soon found that he cannot be friends with both Indians and the Englishwoman: 'one had to choose', and he has chosen the Indians.

He cultivates, with tact and insight, his friendship with Aziz. And here he becomes aware of an inadequacy in himself. As Aziz shows him the photograph of his wife, he wonders whether the kindness he can offer this 'queer nation' is enough or whether it does not require what he cannot give, 'an occasional intoxication of the blood'. Moreover he has such a poor crop of secrets to share. He contemplates his own moderation and realizes that he will not be intimate with anyone. Finally his experience at Chandrapore tests his rather easily held convictions and elicits from him a capacity for intimate friendship.

He defends and supports Aziz, with moderation and good sense indeed, but also with courage. While he regrets taking sides he sees the necessity for it. His refusal to stand when Ronny enters the Club is the gesture of commitment. Again, immediately following this act he experiences a sense of discontent. The charm of the Marabar Hills and of the sky cannot touch him. He wonders whether he is 'truly successful as a human being' and his equilibrium, his Western control, suddenly seems unsatisfying. Perhaps he should have been working at something else all his life. He feels sad.

A harsher sadness grips him as he attends the 'grim little function' of his reappearance at the Club. The 'echo' seems to dominate the world and spread over it. It belongs to the 'universe that he had missed or rejected'. He feels lost. The dinner with Aziz that follows is not successful and he feels now that it is not so easy to 'travel light' when affection is involved. His letter to Aziz explaining his outburst at Aziz's ponderous probings about Adela misfires too.

At the end of the book, returning home to England, Fielding finds relief in the formal harmony of the Mediterranean world, delight in the English June. So his moderate liberalism has been tested, explored, deepened. He encounters and fights racial prejudice, and discovers within himself both inadequacies and an unexpected capacity for affection, love. He meets, too, the power of evil, frustrating in its evasiveness. Then the old claims of Western Europe and of England come to him refreshingly.

Mrs Moore

She had come to that state where the horror of the universe and its smallness are both visible at the same time – the twilight of the double vision in which so many elderly people are involved.

There is difficulty in discussing Mrs Moore as a character in the novel. She is finally, it seems, more an emblem or a vehicle: she 'stands for' the possibility, the hope of true accord between Indian and English; she records the apathy and despair that invade the human soul as its struggles in a hostile environment. She is one of the people of instinctive wisdom who, in Forster's novels, both understand and suffer more than others. She has much in common with Mrs Wilcox of *Howard's End* and Mrs Emerson of *Room with a View*.

Nevertheless this larger, more impersonal significance emerges only as the novel develops; in the early chapters at least she is, quite realistically, an elderly English widow visiting India with a girl who will probably marry her son by her first husband. She has worldly wisdom and a habit of resignation: 'she . . . had learnt that Life never gives us what we want at the moment that we consider appropriate.' She is 'stupefied' by the Club with its narrowness and prejudice; and evokes an eager response in Aziz when, meeting her by chance at the mosque, he discovers she is 'different'. Outside, after *Cousin Kate* is over, she feels 'a sudden sense of unity, of kinship with the heavenly bodies' pass through her. This extends to the small wasp she finds on the tip of her cloak-peg. Love and harmony seem to gather round her. She is out of sympathy with her son

Ronny, and tries to persuade him that he is in India to be pleasant, that a sincere desire to be so will win God's blessing. She fails – and realizes, too, that in some elusive way the mention of God's name has become less efficacious for her since she came to India.

A feeling of apathy envelops her in the days before the Marabar caves outing. The echo of the caves dominates her mind and spirit. She loses faith in 'poor little talkative Christianity'; the 'affectionate and sincere words' that Aziz had spoken seem to belong not to her but to the air.

This spiritual despair conquers her completely. She is resentful and irritable; she is aware that Adela needs help but is unwilling to offer any. And she is aware that Aziz is innocent, but she appears to be indifferent. She accepts Ronny's 'excellent notion' that she should return to England, but without enthusiasm. She is indeed drained of all power, all desire. She suffers, since the experiences of the caves, the 'twilight of the double vision' in which we can 'neither act nor refrain from action, we can neither ignore nor respect infinity'. The 'abyss', she has discovered, is 'petty'. As she travels across India a flicker of life comes; but it tells her only that she has not seen the 'right places', that she was wrong in taking the echo as 'final'. She dies at sea, her body being lowered into 'yet another India'.

She then lives on: in the minds of the Chandrapore natives as a kind of legend; in the mind of Godbole as someone of profound spiritual importance; in the mind of Aziz as someone of infinite sympathy, whose memory, evoked by her son, can make the past live vividly again for him. It is the trip on the lake, which Aziz's full heart leads him to take, that brings about the final reconciliation – pathetically limited as it is – between Aziz and Fielding.

Godbole

Covered with grease and dust, Professor Godbole had once more developed the life of his spirit.

Professor Godbole is 'polite and enigmatic'; like Mrs Moore, he has access to sources of wisdom that the other characters do not share. Unlike Mrs Moore his aloofness from the clash of wills and people, round which the novel centres, comes from a spiritual serenity. His whole appearance – grey moustache, grey-blue eyes, fair complexion, turban the colour of pale purple macaroni – suggests harmony, a harmony between East and West. The elusiveness, the evasiveness that strikes harshly at other points in the novel here becomes something calm and restful. His thin voice gives out sounds that, to the Western ear, are unintelligible, like the 'song of an unknown bird'; only the servants who cluster round understand it. Its 'message', too, is enigmatic: the milkmaiden, who is Godbole, calls to Krishna to come, but he does not come – he 'neglects to come', even, it seems, in another song (though one is not quite sure of this, for Godbole may have misunderstood Mrs Moore's question).

Forster draws this character with humorous love. Godbole will not give Fielding a straightforward opinion on whether he thinks Aziz guilty or no; astounds him by asking if the (disastrous) expedition to the Marabar caves was a 'successful one'; asserts that he, of course, could have no opinion because he was not present. Then he deviates into a discussion on the best name for his High School; looks 'sly and charming' when Fielding poses a question bluntly; speaks with an air of 'daring and coyness' of the universal presence of evil; and concludes the conversation with a lengthy account of a legend that culminates, characteristically, in a cow.

His integrity is of a non-Western kind (perhaps specifically Hindu): Aziz taxes him with holding back the truth about Fielding's marriage and has to be deprecatingly assured that Godbole is, 'as far as my limitations permit, your true friend'. In the ceremony at Mau, in the closing section of the novel, Godbole develops 'the life of the spirit'; here is evoked the vision of unity that Fielding and Aziz, on a different plane, struggle towards and that the novel never completely rejects. Godbole sees again Mrs Moore: he is a Brahman, she a Christian whom Aziz had claimed as 'a Moslem'. Through a trick of memory or telepathy the scene in which she had spoken lovingly to the wasp comes to his mind and, through the 'faintly clinging forms of trouble' that surround her, he reveres 'One old Englishwoman and one little, little wasp.'

Adela

Disaster had shown her her limitations.

Forster draws with painful accuracy the callow eagerness of Adela to see the real India; her earnest but loveless struggling to make contact with Indians; her forthright desire to 'get things straight' with Ronny; her suffering under the stress of her experience in the cave and the insistent echo. She emerges, from her callowness and her ordeal, as someone different, more aware of the complexities of things and of her own limitations. She offers telepathy as an explanation of Mrs Moore's understanding but soon withdraws the 'pert meagre word'. She is 'at the end of her spiritual tether' and she is aware of this as she would not have been before.

Minor characters

The novel has not the exuberant variety of minor characters that one finds in a novel by Dickens but there are many people sketched briefly and succinctly. *Major Turton* carries out his duties efficiently and without love, without respect for those he governs; *Mrs Turton* reveals her ignorance, not only by her verbs, which are confined to the imperative mood; *Ronny* tries eagerly and successfully to adopt the manners and ideas of the Turtons and *Callendars*; *Hamidullah* remembers with nostalgia his days in an English country rectory; The *Nawab Bahadur* behaves with dignity; *Macbride* airs his theory of climatic zones; *Dr Panna Lal*, 'of ignoble origin', skips like a goat, scuttles like a hen and averts disaster.

Chapter summaries, textual notes and revision questions

Part 1 Mosque

The Dedication

Forster met Syed Ross Mahood in 1907. 'Until I met him India was a vague jumble of rajahs, sahibs, babus and elephants . . . He made everything real and exciting as soon as he began to talk, and seventeen years later when I wrote *Passage to India* I dedicated it to him out of gratitude as well as love, for it could never have been written without him.' *Two Cheers for Democracy*, p. 256. *The chapter titles that follow are not Forster's, but have been supplied by the editor as a help to students.*

Chapter 1, Caves and city and sky

The Marabar Caves, the scene of the crucial incident in the novel, are introduced in the very first line; they are extraordinary. Then one sees Chandrapore. Note the tone of disgust in 'swelling here, shrinking there, like some low but indestructible form of life': a note that recurs throughout the novel, infrequently, but bringing a note of distress sharper than the general tenor of the novel leads one to expect. Viewed from the civil station the city seems very different. This ambivalent, fluctuating note is central to the novel: things are not what they seem to be, or appear differently in different circumstances (for example the central episode in the cave).

The civil station 'provokes no emotion': it is neutral. Only the 'overarching sky' is common to it and the city. The sky, too, is powerful – 'it settles everything'. Recall this as the novel progresses, and as it draws to its close.

Note the picture of the Marabar Hills, 'thrusting' their way upwards. They are, indeed, 'extraordinary'.

Maidan An open space in or near a town; a kind of esplanade or parade ground.

Chapter 2, At Hamidullah's and in the mosque

There is a note of gaiety in the opening, an air of relaxation, as the Indians discuss whether or not it is possible to be friends with an Englishman. Now a note of unreality is introduced, for the servants' shout that dinner is ready is understood, correctly, to mean that they wished it were. Hugh Bannister has apparently succumbed to the Anglo-Indians. The mood of the discussion changes, and they recall small courtesies. Note the irony of the phrase 'angelic ministrations' by which Forster describes these small courtesies, an irony that reflects on both English and Indian: one is condescending, the other too deferential. Note the extravagant politeness of Hamidullah Begum as she prolongs her remarks.

Aziz begins to quote poetry. Note his favourite themes, and the delight with which the whole group listens to 'words, words'. Mohammed Latif and a servant manipulate the bicycle – over a tintack! Aziz leaves 'with unexpected energy'. He does, finally, clean his teeth!

He receives 'the inevitable snub'; walks over the hostile soil; and turns into the mosque to rest. It symbolizes Islam to him – a faith in which his body and soul are at ease. He responds, characteristically, to the pathos of the inscription. He meets Mrs Moore and at once a 'flame' of sympathy flares up between them. Aziz claims her as an Oriental. He walks away in a mood of serene self-sufficiency.

hookah A pipe with a long flexible tube; the smoke is drawn through water contained in a vase.

Islam The latest of the monotheistic religions, based on the teachings of Mohammed, the Arab prophet AD 570—632. The basic tenet is, 'There is no God but Allah, and Mohammed is his prophet.'
chuprassi An attendant or messenger.
pan The betel-leaf; hence the combination of betel-leaf and arecanut, lime, etc. used as a chewing substance.
tonga A small, light two-wheeled carriage.
ablution-tank The tank near the entrance of the mosque for the ritual ablution.

Chapter 3, The English

Consider the air of disenchantment that enfolds both Adela and Mrs Moore. Mrs Moore takes this less seriously; she realizes that 'Adventures do occur, but not punctually.' Notice the gentle irony, touching lightly on the callow eagerness of Adela. Turton voices his approval of Heaslop. The National Anthem follows, bringing stiffening of the will. Then another round of drinks. This is the trite world of amateur dramatics (*Cousin Kate*), in which individuals quickly become merely members of the group. Each day follows its stiff, deadening routine.

Turton suggests a 'Bridge Party'. The Turtons are little gods here; but their retirement will be much less regal. Adela is persistent; Ronny complacently patient; he understands 'why she did not understand'.

Outside, Mrs Moore feels 'a sudden sense of unity, of kinship with the heavenly bodies'. Note the delicate metaphor conveying the 'strange freshness' that this experience leaves in her. Ronny is 'scratchy and dictatorial' when he realizes that his mother has been talking to an Indian: he is unsure in his, as yet, second-hand pronouncements. Mrs Moore feels that Ronny has misrepresented Aziz; he had 'slain' his 'essential life'. It is this 'essential life' that Mrs Moore can instinctively understand and feel for. She looks lovingly at the small wasp. The night is uneasy.

Notice how the novel moves here from the world of social interchange to that of solitary meditation, and then to the sky and stars.

mem-sahib A title used (or once used) by the natives of India in addressing European women.
sahib A respectful title similarly used in addressing an Englishman or a European. Hence, in European terminology (as here) a true Englishman, 'the right sort'.
pukka A genuine, true. Again, this implies approval of a person as being the 'right type'. Adela was not!
Benares The holy city of India.
hakim Physician or doctor; here, apparently, some kind of quack.

Chapter 4, Response to the invitation

Consider and carefully define the differing reactions to the invitation. This social act has caused much perturbation in the unreal, unnatural situation in which English and Indian find themselves. Note Forster's glance at those who 'had not received a card from Mr Turton'; and at the circles beyond these – 'humanity grading and drifting beyond the educated vision, until no earthly invitation can embrace it'. This is an instance of the generosity of Forster's vision, its scope and its compassion, and it is also a notice to the reader that the scope of his *novel* is limited – it embraces only the 'educated vision'.

Forster looks ironically at the missionaries. *They* are troubled by the problem of the diversity and immensity of mankind, but leave to heaven any moves towards unity; there alone will the 'incompatible multitudes' be reconciled. But there must, it seems, be some limit to 'the divine hospitality'; and Mr Sorley becomes uneasy 'during the descent to the wasps'. Forster mocks them gently. Mrs Moore is stirred to affection by the wasp: 'pretty dear'.

the Koran The sacred book of Islam.
Nawab The title of a Moslem official who acted as deputy governor of a province.

Chapter 5, The Bridge Party; Mrs Moore and Ronny

Ronny and Mrs Turton confer. European dress had 'lighted like a leprosy' on the Indians. Words fade away beneath the 'impartial' sky. Beyond the sky there is something else, perhaps even more impartial. As one contemplates the receding infinite vision (and we recall the 'overarching sky' of the first chapter), Forster returns to the mundane – to the world of the 'educated vision' which his art can explore.

The scene is humorous and sad: the group of Indian ladies with their 'faces pressed into a bank of shrubs'; the collision with the hollyhocks; Mrs Turton's imperative verbs – and the frustration of Adela as she 'strives in vain against the echoing walls of their civility'.

Turton's behaviour is perfunctory, yet the party is not wholly pointless: the humbler Indians are grateful for the notice bestowed on them; the Nawab Bahadur is aware of the difficulties in the way of such an occasion; Mahmoud Ali's cynicism is tempered by the fascination of having entered the 'shrine' and by the prospect of caricaturing it afterwards. Tennis makes the barrier between the races 'impenetrable'. Adela has a bleak vision of her married life, its stereotyped pattern. Ronny and his mother talk. She suffers quiet distress as she probes and discovers his rigid prejudice: the English posing as gods. Ronny utters his creed. He asserts with gusto that he 'was not in India to behave pleasantly'. He, and the others, lack that 'true regret' that would have 'made him a different man, and the British Empire a different institution'.

Ronny disengages from the interchange when Mrs Moore mentions God, religion having nothing to do, he feels, with life. Mrs Moore has found God persistently in her thoughts since she entered India, yet, paradoxically, his name has never been less efficacious than it is now.

Note how images of the arch (an apparently never ending sequence) and of the echo (with a silence beyond the remotest one) occur again here – as Mrs Moore meets frustration, finding certainty elusive.

purdah A curtain, especially one used to screen women from the sight of men or strangers. Hence the system of such seclusion.
Mohurram A Moslem festival, held during the first ten days of the first month of the Moslem year.
Parsi A descendant of those Persians who fled to India from Persia to escape the Moslem persecution, and who still retain their religion.
Rani A Rajah's wife.
gram A dwarf species of pea (apparently tart in flavour).
Maharani The wife of a maharajah.
Native State A state ruled over by a native prince and retaining, under fairly loose British control, some kind of independence. This is, of course, the situation existing in 1924. Then India was under the single control of Great Britain, exercised loosely with the Native States or more directly with the larger part of the country. With independence in 1947 came 'partition', into two states – India and Pakistan.

Chapter 6, Mainly Aziz

Note the exact description of Aziz's attitude towards his profession, the mingling of professional and personal manners of conduct. Aziz reacts with amusement to Callendar's outburst of temper; but his amusement lacks 'fundamental gaiety'. He meditates on his dead wife. He wavers in his opinion as to an after-life; and 'the corpuscles of his blood' decide which opinion he holds at which moment. (For instance he did not change his mind about going to the party; 'it changed itself'.) Self-pity (he is fond of pathos) and genuine sorrow mingle as he contemplates the photograph. His character – mercurial, impulsive, fragile – is conveyed with a delicate incisive sympathy.

The good fellowship of the polo encounter soon fades; and, poignantly, each carries away the same delusive thought. (We meet the subaltern, briefly, later in the novel.)

Aziz and Dr Panna Lal quarrel. Aziz becomes anxious, 'breathing the prevalent miasma' of power. So, alien domination affects, distorts human relationships over a wide area, not simply that of the Indian/English contact. Anxieties, prejudices, little meannesses, thrive in the unnatural atmosphere.

tonga See note p. 51
tum-tum Dog-cart.
chukker A period of play in polo. In *My Early Life* Winston Churchill describes the idyllic days in the Indian Army round about the turn of the century, days in which polo figured very prominently.
Mecca Mohammed's birthplace. The chief shrine of Islam and the object of pilgrimage.
Brahma The supreme god of the Hindu religion, with Vishnu and Shiva forming the Trinity.

Chapter 7, Fielding and the tea-party

Forster sketches Fielding's character. He believes in the interchange of ideas, a creed inappropriate to Chandrapore. He has to make a choice between the Indians and English women – the two 'would not combine'.

Aziz wrenches off his collar-stud and lends it to Fielding, a gesture of excessive, ludicrous courtesy. He senses Fielding's 'fundamental good-will'. Note the metaphor which now follows; and consider how this novel deals, in fact, with individuals who 'grapple beneath the shifting tides of emotion', and how some reach an 'anchorage' and some are 'carried on to the rocks'.

Aziz's attitude towards Adela remains 'straightforward'; beauty would have 'troubled him', but he is not troubled. Note the dialogue concerning 'mystery and muddle'; 'muddle' is a recurrent motif in the novel. Aziz's face grows tender as they discuss the widow; he is tender towards almost everyone, even towards the English who, he feels, cannot help being so 'cold'. Adela misinterprets Aziz. He is not so enlightened as she thinks him; she assesses him, wrongly, by her own European standards. Professor Godbole arrives. Note Adela's 'important remark', occurring without premeditation, almost subconsciously: it reveals to her a decision she had already made, without, perhaps, realizing that she had made it.

Aziz gives his impulsive invitation. Aziz and Godbole engage in their strange dialogue. Adela is unaware of its real meaning. Ronny brusquely and rudely intervenes. Aziz, his nerves jarred, becomes provocative. Professor Godbole sings, and then explains his song.

The chapter ends in silence and peace.

Mogul A Muslim dynasty founded in Delhi, in 1562. The empire reached its peak of power under Shah Jahan and Aurangzeb, but was in decline when conquered by the British in 1803.

the Peacock Throne Inside the palace at Delhi, built during the reign of Shah Jahan.

Post-Impressionism A movement in modern painting largely motivated by a reaction against Impressionism and its concern with the purely visual.

Brahman A member of the highest Hindu caste. One mark of Hinduism is a very elaborate caste system. See note on 'Brahma', p. 55.

Krishna The Hindu god of fire and light. In legend Krishna is a beautiful youth brought up among cowherds to save him from relatives who seek his death. Many stories relate his exploits with the milkmaids.

Chapter 8, Adela and Ronny; the accident and its consequences

Ronny gets on Adela's nerves; she sees his limitations. They have 'a thorough talk'. Ronny responds generously to Adela's rejection of him (where his compatriots were concerned he was generous). It is difficult to identify the green bird (p. 101); certainty is elusive in India. They go for a drive in the Nawab Bahadur's car; and a 'spurious unity' descends on them. Only the darkness seems durable, but this too is spurious, for it is modified by the gleams of the dawn that 'leaked up round the edges of the world', and by the starlight. There is an acrid, disillusioned air about this episode.

An air of indistinctness surrounds the accident, too. Was it hyena or buffalo? Adela withdraws what she had said to Ronny; and the (unforeseen) consequence of their engagement follows.

Ronny, Adela and Mrs Moore dine together. Ronny recounts his day, a satisfactory one. Mrs Moore conjectures a ghost as the cause of the accident; and, in a desultory way, Adela harks back to the half-heard remark as they play patience. Meanwhile the distress of the Nawab Bahadur, visited by 'ghosts' of his past, is communicated to and shared by his own people. Again, the races are distinct, some experiences cannot be shared.

Note, in the last paragraph, the deliberate distancing of these events. The players go to bed; in other parts of the globe other people, so remote from these, awaken. The night wears on. The chapter ends on an ominous note.

nullah Stream, river; watercourse.
peon Attendant, orderly.

Chapter 9, Aziz: his illness; his plans; his visitors

Aziz hears two sets of bells. Their music differs, so do their audiences. Forster describes Aziz's rational attitude towards his sexual desires, and the nature of the conventions by which he is ruled. Visitors arrive. Hamidullah quickly dampens sprouting suspicions. Aziz recites poetry; and the listeners are 'overwhelmed by its pathos'. Note the gentle irony of Forster ('a poem should touch the hearer with a sense of his own weakness, and should institute some comparison between mankind and flowers'), and his acute regard for a civilization that has not divorced itself from literature. They listen with pleasure, without embarrassment. Hamidullah dwells nostalgically on his life in Cambridge – 'another poem that had ended'. He regrets the passing of those days when 'politics had not mattered'.

Fielding arrives and refuses to become involved in a theoretical discussion as to whether he should hold a post that Indians could occupy. His persistence in regarding only the actual instance and rejoicing in the fact that he himself is happy to be in India at that particular moment disconcerts the company – they seek some passing tribute to Morality and Justice. Fielding prepares to leave, rather disappointed with the encounter. Has he been simply 'making himself cheap'?

saddhus Corruption of 'Siddh', a holy man.
Ghalib A Moslem poet, died 1869. An inspiration to the generation of the Indian Mutiny, whose outlook grew more patriotic.
punkah A large swinging fan made of cloth, suspended from the ceiling and worked by a cord.

Chapter 10, The heat

In the oppressive heat the world of animals comes into its own. Human self-esteem is injured; people take refuge in their bungalows. They are aware of 'a vague threat'. The sun is bright, but the brightness is drowned in excess of light and there is no glory.

In this chapter Forster suspends human action for a

while (note where Chapter 9 ends and Chapter 11 begins); the universe continues its processes. There is a sense of unease.

Chapter 11, Aziz and Fielding

Distressed at the state of his house, Aziz makes a gesture of atonement, of friendship. He praises Fielding's kindness: it is kindness that Indians need. He shows Fielding the photograph of his wife, because he has 'nothing else to show'. It is a gesture and a commitment.

Fielding examines his own life and finds it fundamentally unsatisfactory. Where was 'the occasional intoxication of the blood'? Adela is mentioned in relation to marriage. Aziz is charmed by Fielding's notion of 'travelling light'; Fielding utters his 'creed'. Aziz, alone, meditates on Fielding's lack of wisdom. Now, drifting on the tide of emotion, his mood has become patronizing. But, finally, happy memories of the last two hours accompany him into sleep.

chunam Plaster.
tazia A model of the tomb of Ali (son-in-law of Mohammed) and Husain (son of Ali). Apparently of some height.

Revision questions on Part 1

1 What does (*a*) the mosque and (*b*) his encounter there with Mrs Moore mean to Aziz?
2 Discuss the motives which led to the Bridge Party, the reactions of the Indians to the invitation and the Bridge Party itself.
3 Write a brief account of Fielding's tea-party (Ch. 7), focusing on the relationships that grow and are revealed between the different people there.

4 Trace the (changing) relationship between Adela and Ronny.
5 Trace the growing friendship between Aziz and Fielding, noticing how it develops in different ways within the two different characters.
6 Describe the friction that exists between Ronny and Mrs Moore, and examine its causes.
7 Note the occasions in which 'muddle' and confusion occur.

Part 2 Caves

Chapter 12, The Marabar Hills and Caves

Forster looks at the very ancient hills of Southern India, 'the high places of the Dravidia'. The caves of the Marabar Hills, he says, are easy to describe. But this refers only to their dimensions and their surface appearance, for there is something elusive about them. Human speech cannot define their character. Little light penetrates into their interior, the circular chamber. As the visitor strikes a match, two flames, the actual one and its reflection in the highly polished walls 'are seen'. But the effort fails; local rumour speaks of other more mysterious caves, without entrances. There is one of these, it is said, within the boulder that is perched precariously on the summit of Kawa Dol.

Here, in this evocative chapter, Forster again 'distances' his whole action. Things are seen against the background of geological time. This immense antiquity gives a feeling of mystery (but unromantic mystery), strangeness mingling with horror, to the hills and to the caves in which the central, but never clearly solved, episode of the novel occurs. The episode, like the caves, is 'dark', and, like the undiscovered caves, empty of meaning.

the Dravidia The Dravidian language, probably spoken over most of India until it was over-run by Indo-European invaders in the second millenium BC. Now spoken over the greater part of southern India.
Buddha Guatama Buddha (563—483 BC), founder of the philosophico-religious system of Buddhism.
the Bo tree The tree under which Buddha sat for weeks in profound meditation. It is called the Tree of Intelligence.

Chapter 13, Departure

Adela's casual remark travels and grows. Aziz hastily arranges the outing, which he had relegated to the back of his mind. No one has any enthusiasm for the outing, but it is to take place. Aziz has many problems to face, for 'he has challenged the spirit of the Indian earth, which tries to keep men in compartments.' An air of confusion and scrappiness surrounds the (very) early morning preparations. Forster catches the note of desultory and yet chaotic progress. Day comes rather hesitantly – and thoroughly unromantically: 'The night was still dark, but had acquired the temporary look that indicates its end'. Mohammed Latif acts (willingly) as a stooge. Fielding misses the train and Aziz is distraught. Adela and Mrs Moore act kindly; Aziz recovers. The countryside and the sky are brought to one's mind. Aziz wonders why he is taking his party to see the caves.

tiffin A light meal, especially of curried dishes and fruit.
purdah See note p. 54.
pujah religious rite.

Chapter 14, The Caves: Mrs Moore loses faith

Forster speaks of the usual dullness of life, the human spirit slumbering for most of the time 'inside its cocoon of work'. Mrs Moore and Adela have been apathetic for a fortnight.

Mrs Moore accepts her apathy, but Adela, expecting more, does not. She tries to get Mrs Moore interested in her plans. But Mrs Moore, experiencing either 'vision or nightmare', remains apathetic. Adela takes refuge in thoughts of her future. She ignores the message (boredom? futility?) of the train, while the 'real India', which she had thought she wanted to see, remains outside the periphery of her vision. The dawn promises to be magnificent, but 'at the supreme moment . . . nothing occurred'. Adela again takes refuge in her thoughts, this time in memories of Grasmere. Grasmere was both romantic *and* tidy. The train arrives, and the elephant is there. The train wobbles back through the fields.

An odd stillness occurs; and air of hallucination and foreboding descends; everything seems 'cut off at its root and therefore infected with illusion'. There is confusion ('muddle') over a snake – confusion but no romance. Aziz feels the happiness of successful hospitality, and the purer pleasure of selfless delight in his guests' pleasure. He speaks of his ancestors. Adela seeks his advice, confides in him regarding her fear of becoming like the other Anglo-Indians. She is too outspoken for Aziz and the conversation – a little civilized world they had created – breaks up. Notice the air of distaste, verging on horror, that pervades the paragraph beginning 'The first cave was tolerably convenient.' Here is an environment in which more than social errors and confusion will occur. Mrs Moore is oppressed by the crush and the stench – and the echo. She withdraws from further explorings. The echo begins to 'undermine her hold on life'; it denies all spiritual values; she is terrified. The words of Aziz are lost in the air.

nullah See note p. 57.
the Taj The mosque of Taj Mahal, left as a monument to his beloved dead wife by Shah Jahan.
shawm A musical instrument of the oboe type.

Grasmere One of the smaller lakes of the English Lake District.
shikar Hunting.
Parvati He personifies power.
Alamgir Aurangzeb, the last of the great Moguls.
Babur Founder of the Mogul Empire. He died in 1530.
Akbar The greatest of the Mogul Emperors.

Chapter 15, The Caves; Adela realizes something

They continue an expedition that is now 'slightly tedious'. Aziz is concerned over some signs of disorganization in his party; Adela is pre-occupied with thoughts of her forthcoming marriage to Ronny. She realizes that they do not love each other, and wonders whether she should break off the engagement. She speaks of marriage to Aziz. He is shocked by her inquiry as to whether he has more than one wife, and plunges into a cave to cover his confusion. Adela enters another cave.

Chapter 16, The Caves and the arrest

Aziz seeks Adela but cannot find her. He catches a glimpse of her far below. Fielding arrives and is annoyed when he hears that Adela has left. In his confusion over Adela's tactless inquiries, Aziz tells 'a good many lies'. Fielding is annoyed and anxious. They return to Chandrapore (the Marabar Hills, now at a distance, seem 'finite and rather romantic'). Aziz is arrested.

topi An Indian sun-helmet made from the pith of the sola plant.
howdah A seat to contain two or more people on the back of an elephant.

Chapter 17, Turton's reaction

Turton's face is 'white, fanatical, and rather beautiful'. He is 'half mad himself'; and his words of reproach to Fielding seem 'to fill the waiting room with their staleness and ungenerosity'. His mind is set on revenge. He looks sternly at Fielding because the Principal is keeping his head (while 'the herd had decided on emotion'). His sense of justice still functions and he quells the rioters.

There is no irony in Forster's description; nor is there any sympathy (in the sense of feeling *with* someone). But there is understanding – an understanding that makes his condemnation, his moral disgust, all the more penetrating.

chuprassi Attendant or henchman.

Chapter 18, Macbride and 'toeing the line'

Notice the brief sketch of Macbride's character – and his theory of climatic zones. Macbride is, to a degree, rational; but he is also prejudiced. Surely 'two sahibs' should stand together and 'pool all they know'. He is out of tune with Fielding's feelings and cannot bring himself into tune with them. He refuses Fielding permission to see Adela. (Note Fielding's reason for wishing to see her: to hear her story himself, to provide a different audience.) Meanwhile 'the opposite army' gathers.

the Mutiny records The Mutiny of 1857.
Bhavagad Gita Bhagavatism is the religion of the incarnations of Vishnu. This poem is the *Song of the Lord*, the chief literary expression of this religion.

Chapter 19, Fielding and Godbole

Fielding is disappointed with Hamidullah, as he temporizes and seems to lack faith in Aziz's innocence. Hamidullah favours Amritrao as lawyer for the defence. Fielding finds that he has to take sides; he regrets this – he had wished to 'slip through India unlabelled', and he foresees 'muddle' on top of the tragedy. There follows the 'queer, vague talk' with Godbole (who hopes the expedition was successful!), then probes Fielding about the best name for his projected new school. He is 'sly and charming' and 'looks shyly down the sleeves of his coat'. He speaks of good and evil as both aspects of the Lord and then wonders whether Fielding had time to see any interesting Marabar antiquities. Fielding receives his account of the legend in silence.

So Fielding, seeking with rational intensity to establish Aziz's innocence, discovers that the minds of his Indian friends are working in ways that are either uncongenial or incomprehensible.

pargana Subdivision of a district.

Chapter 20, Fielding at the Club

The Englishwomen feel 'an exalted emotion'; selfish considerations are put aside – for a while. There is an air of deliberate composure. Turton addresses the company in the Club. His mind is full of 'contradictory impulses'; it is a tiring effort to remind himself that Aziz is not yet found guilty. An intoxicating glow fills the others, and they surrender to it. The subaltern of the brief polo encounter with Aziz appears again. Callendar taunts Fielding and spreads vile rumours. Fielding sees evil spreading, propagating itself, and understands the feeling of helplessness that Aziz and Hamidullah experienced. Fielding, refusing to stand when Ronny enters, explicitly commits himself to the side of Aziz. It is, he feels, an unsatisfactory symbol of his commitment (he has nothing personally against Heaslop) but 'there it was, muddled through'.

He looks at the Marabar Hills, gracious in their beauty,

but he experiences nothing. He has a feeling of discontent, dissatisfaction with himself and his life.

Pallas Athene Greek goddess; the defender of Athens and the personification of wisdom.
Gurkhas The dominant racial group of Nepal; hence Nepalese generally. The British had for long recruited troops from among them.
Monsalvat An alternative for Montserrat in Spain, once thought to have been the site of the castle of the Holy Grail.
Walhalla Usually Valhalla; in Norse mythology the home of those killed in battle.

(*Note how Chapters 17–20 and the following chapter describe the odyssey of Fielding among Indians and English.*)

Chapter 21, Fielding; Mohurram; Godbole

Fielding has no regrets about breaking with the Club. Mohurram is 'working up'; and so is the campaign. Godbole, with characteristic knack, has slipped away.

Chapter 22, Adela, Ronny and Mrs Moore

Adela suffers physically and mentally. She oscillates between hard commonsense and hysteria. She feels an acute sense of insult and then a deep sense of guilt. Her intellect assures her that she has no need to be guilty and so she is set again on 'her sterile round'. Mrs Moore, the one person whom she wishes to see, keeps away. She feels that 'evil is loose'. Ronny and Macbride visit her; inform her of the riots; and that Fielding is siding with Aziz. Adela has, again, a vision of her Anglo-Indian future.

As Ronny drives her back to his bungalow the day 'swells like a monster at both ends'. It is oppressive. She finds Mrs Moore sullen. She refuses to 'explain' the echo to Adela: if Adela does not know, it is no good telling her.

Mrs Moore frets, speaks resentfully of the fuss over love and marriage. Adela suddenly feels that she has made a mistake over Aziz and that he is innocent. She feels that Mrs Moore has said so, or rather has uttered the idea rather than the words. Ronny asks his mother whether she has, in fact, said anything of the kind. Casually she expresses her conviction of Aziz's innocence. Ronny speaks of the machinery that has been set in motion. He has an excellent idea.

the Minto Hospital After Lord Minto (1847–1914), Viceroy of India, 1905–10.

Unto us a Son is born The Biblical words have a negative ring here, issuing harshly from Mrs Moore's irritation and despondency.

Chapter 23, Mrs Moore leaves India

Lady Mellanby goes into action; Ronny is gratified. Mrs Moore suffers 'the twilight of the double vision'; she has had a vision, but not a profound one – even, perhaps, a 'petty' one. Her train threads its way through India. She feels that she has failed to make contact. The palm trees mock her as she departs. The chapter ends on a note of bathos.

Chapter 24, The Trial

In the stifling heat of an Indian April people retreat from the sun. Adela prays; she has resumed the habit, for it seems 'the shortest and easiest cut to the unseen'. The Turtons come to collect her; she tells them her echo has returned. Turton reassures her, but keeps from her his knowledge of the long train of appeals that will inevitably follow. They gather, with others, in Ronny's private room at the Court. In the conversation that follows Callendar and Mrs Turton reveal their viciousness.

Their case is called; the court is crowded and very hot; Adela is impressed by the splendid aloofness of the man who pulls the punkah. Macbride develops his case, laboriously and coolly. The English party gather on the platform, but then have to relinquish their position. Macbride mentions Mrs Moore, and Mahmoud Ali is enraged. He quits the court. The legend of 'Esmiss Esmoor' begins.

Adela gives her evidence, fearing exposure of her 'private failure' and speaking not from ordinary memory but from a kind of sense of being then present in the Marabar Hills. She speaks across a 'sort of darkness'. At the crucial moment she wavers; finally she withdraws her charge. The Court breaks up in uproar. The 'beautiful naked god' continues to pull the punkah.

The 'epoch-making' trial of Aziz, with the courtroom scene that is richly comic as well as bitterly sad, the personalities of the Indians and the British and their contrasting national characteristics – all are brilliantly portrayed by Forster. The whole crucial chapter is indeed a *tour de force* by the author.

Balder In Scandinavian mythology the god of light, son of Odin and Frigg.

Persephone In Greek and Roman mythology the goddess of the earth's produce, especially corn. She was carried off to the underworld by Pluto, but ultimately was allowed to spend six months of the year on earth – a nature myth corresponding to the growth of the fruits of the earth in spring and summer.

Lakshmi '. . . born from the churning of the sea and sprinkled with the Ganges by elephants with golden ewers . . .' Lowe's *Encyclopaedia of Mythology*.

he encouraged the Boy Scout movement for seditious reasons Ironic, since nationalist movements have often regarded the Boy Scout movement as a typical Imperialist institution.

Andamans The prison on the Andaman Islands, in the Indian Ocean.
Jain Belonging to the religion originated or perhaps reformed by a contemporary of Buddha, Mahivira, 599–527 BC.

Chapter 25, Confusion and then calm

In the confusion Fielding and Adela are transported, in a victoria, to the grounds of Government College. Aziz longs for Cyril's presence. The mood of the crowd is ugly; disaster is averted by the pathetic clownings of Dr Panna Lal, who has been 'mislaid'. The heat stupefies, and night comes.

the victoria A light, low four-wheeled carriage with a collapsible hood, seats for two people and an elevated seat in front for the driver.
sais Groom.
landau A four-wheeled carriage, with a top in two parts so that it may be closed or partly open or entirely open.

Chapter 26, Adela at the Government College

Adela and Fielding are having one of their 'numerous curious interviews'. Adela explains the feeling of being ill-at-ease, of 'living at half-pressure', which descended on her just about the time of Fielding's tea-party. They discuss ghosts, and fear the dead 'don't live again'. Hamidullah is displeased to find Adela there. He is full of bitterness against her: she had shown no emotion in court and so his imagination and generosity had not been evoked. She lacked, indeed, the spontaneous warmth that the Oriental mind required. While Adela goes to speak to Ronny, Fielding and Hamidullah speak of the death of Mrs Moore: to them it is a passing incident – they had 'invested their emotions elsewhere'. Ronny and Adela enter. Fielding decides that Adela should stay at the College. Later the question of compensation arises. Fielding loses his 'usual sane view of human intercourse'.

Note the rumours that later collect around this episode and those following.

band-ghari Again, a type of vehicle.

Chapter 27, Fielding and Aziz

After the Victory Banquet the revellers relax on the roof of the Nawab Bahadur's (now plain Mr Zulfiquar's) house. They experience the blessings of leisure that the West cannot know. There is grace, elegance and civilization in their movements and gestures. Fielding tries to persuade Aziz to drop his claim for compensation. Aziz finally says that he will consult Mrs Moore. Fielding has then to reveal to him that she is dead. Aziz cannot accept this. Mrs Moore, Fielding thinks, still eludes him: she possesses a kind of immortality as long as this misunderstanding persists. The 'gracious interlude' closes.

Chapter 28, Mrs Moore's death; and reaction to it

Mrs Moore had 'failed to enter the Mediterranean'. A legend of Mrs Moore flourishes in Chandrapore. Ronny has an uneasy conscience; he stifles it. He feels that Adela must leave, too – part of his callow past that he now rejects.

mater Mother (Latin); the Public School term is satirically fitting here. Ronny joins the Anglo-Indians for good and all.

Chapter 29, Aziz's renunciation and Adela's return

Note the ironic description of Sir Gilbert. Fielding finds himself closely involved with Adela's affairs. His regard for her grows. He defines the reason for her failure. Aziz and his Indian friends are aggressive (while Adela is humble).

Aziz renounces all claims to compensation; he gains no credit with the English for this. Fielding learns that Adela's engagement is broken. They discuss the incident in the cave, and Mrs Moore's instinctive knowledge. They reach spiritual accord. As they part Fielding describes, with powerful compassion, the sense of communion between them and the sense of inadequacy and the air of 'dream' that cuts across their stable lives at this moment.

Adela leaves, pursued by Anthony. The missionary speaks, in the clear light of Port Said, his trite, meaningless words. But Adela 'sees' what she has to do.

Tunbridge Wells and Cheltenham England has these pockets of retired 'Colonial' people, mainly at inland spas and the quieter coastal resorts.

Lesseps The French engineer (1805—94), builder of the Suez Canal.

Chapter 30, Aziz and his plans

A Hindu-Moslem entente begins, as a result of the trial. But a 'half-embrace' typifies the union that will be achieved. Aziz contemplates writing poetry, and is led towards the idea of a motherland. He grows hard; he discusses his future with Hamidullah.

Cordova and Samarkand Moslem cities – of Spain, and of that part of Russia which borders on Afghanistan respectively.

Chapter 31, Coldness between Aziz and Fielding

A tragic coldness develops. Aziz believes the rumours about Fielding and Adela; Fielding reacts with uncontrolled anger. Their relationship is marred. Fielding attends 'the grim little function' in the Club. He is pestered, on the 'verge of his mind', by the power of the echo, its pervasive power. At dinner with Aziz the conversation goes jerkily:

'nothing clicked tight'. Suspicion (co-existing with belief in Fielding's denials) fills the mind of Aziz. Fielding's letter fails to improve things, indeed it jars Aziz's susceptibilities. So the abrasive friction continues, and the friends of Aziz successfully foster his suspicions.

addicted to cameos A cameo is a relief carved in a precious stone (such as onyx, agate etc), having two layers of different colours. Aziz treasures the brief interchange with Fielding; he has a liking for something self-contained, pleasing in miniature. The irony here is gentle.
almeira Cupboard.
durry Small carpet.

Chapter 32, Fielding comes home

There is clarity in Alexandria, as against the intricacies of Bombay. In St Mark's Fielding discovers the 'joys of form', the harmony that exists between man and the earth in a 'civilization that has escaped muddle'. Tender romantic fancies flower again as he reaches England in summer-time.

Here Fielding escapes the insidious, disruptive influence of the Indian 'earth', the earth that seems so unfriendly to man's hopes.

piazetta A small square.
San Giorgio The Church of San Giorgio (16th Century).
St Mark's The basilica of St Mark's, the eleventh-century rebuilding of a ninth-century church.
the Bosphorus The strait in Turkey dividing Europe from Asia. It connects the Black Sea and the Aegean.
the Pillars of Hercules The twin rocks at the western entrance to the Mediterranean. According to Pliny, Hercules tore assunder the rocks which had previously entirely cut off the Mediterranean from the ocean.

Revision questions on Part 2

1 Discuss and carefully define the atmosphere that the Marabar caves generate, and consider the mood that envelops the party as they travel there.
2 Define Mrs Moore's experience of the caves.
3 Describe the reaction of the English community to the episode in the caves and Aziz's arrest.
4 Mr MacBride was 'the most reflective and best educated of the Chandrapore officials'. Show how his words and actions reveal this. How powerful is racial prejudice in him?
5 Show how Forster describes Adela's mind as it pursues its 'sterile round'.
6 How is Mrs Moore's state of mind, following her experience of the caves, described later in Chapter 23?
7 Trace carefully the sequence of events in the actual trial.
8 What are the effects of his experience on Aziz? (Relevant chapters in Part 3 will need to be considered, too, but the general nature of his reaction is made clear in Ch. 30.)
9 Describe the reaction of the Indian community to the news of Aziz's release.
10 Show how Fielding and Adela move towards a fuller understanding of and sympathy with each other.
11 Define the differing reasons and motives for the departures from India of Fielding, Mrs Moore and Adela.
12 At points Fielding's faith and optimism fail him. Trace the movement of his mind in these moments of near-despair.

Part 3 Temple

Chapter 33 God is Love

The ridiculous and the sublime mingle in the Hindu festival at Mau. The crowd seethes 'like a beneficent potion'; music comes from many sources; rain falls; Professor Godbole's pince-nez catches in a jasmine garland; a Europeanized band plays 'Nights of Gladness'; the feeble Rajah is carried out to witness the ceremony of Birth. Amongst this Godbole recalls Mrs Moore – and a wasp he had seen once (One recalls the last few sentences of Chapter 3 p. 55.) The Birth is celebrated, punctually. Godbole dandles the silk napkin, which is and is not the God. The Rajah retires to a room where Aziz awaits him. The festival continues, involving the quality of merriment that Christianity has 'shirked'. Butter is thrown about; the flies awake. The memory of Mrs Moore, with 'faintly clinging forms of trouble', lingers in Godbole's mind.

In an interview with *The Paris Review* – Forster, asked for a comment on this description of the Hindu festival – explains it in terms of the 'shape' of his book; he needed a large block, a lump, at this point in the construction of the novel. He feels that, while the end comes too quickly after this description, the whole account fulfils its purpose. There is, quite clearly, another 'purpose'. Here is the depiction of a spiritual serenity that the West lacks, an all-inclusiveness of mind that it is too 'finicky' to contemplate – slap-stick comedy and flies are part of a religious experience. This is something that Mrs Moore alone of the Europeans understood – an instinctive understanding that explains her sympathy with Aziz, her understanding of what happened (or did not happen) in the cave, her presence in Godbole's mind. The episode, the whole chapter and its related passages, is part of the pattern of meaning in the novel as well as part of its structural shape.

Tukaram An Indian mystical poet who lived in the seventeenth century.
ryot Peasants.
oleograph Picture printed in oils.
Herod and the murder of the Innocents Herod ordered all male children of Bethlehem above the age of two years to be put to death. Matthew, 2, 1–18.

Chapter 34, Fielding's arrival

Aziz is hoping that the floods will prevent Fielding from arriving. Here at Mau he has met a different kind of cleavage, that between Brahman and non-Brahman. (The Indian soil has many fissures: Hinduism is 'riven into sects and clans'.) Aziz has abandoned Western notions of medical discipline; he has, indeed, 'escaped' from the English. And, says Forster, the impulse that led him to do this was sound. Fielding's letter announcing his marriage has been only partly read: Aziz believes the marriage is to Adela. Life passes pleasantly for Aziz. The political climate has changed. In anger Aziz tears up a note Fielding has sent.

bhakti Devotion. The bhakti saints, whose golden age is AD 1000–1800, proclaimed the love that exists between the deity and the human soil.
Plassy A mis-spelt reference to the battle of Plassey, 1757 (see also p. 12 of these Notes). This victory by Robert Clive (1725—74) laid the foundation of British supremacy in India.
bulbuls The bulbul is a bird belonging to the thrush family; it is sometimes called 'the nightingale of the East'.
sanskrit The sacred language of Hinduism.

Chapter 35, They meet again

Aziz walks with his children to the Shrine of the Head (his children so similar to himself). They wander over an old fort. It is revealed that the Rajah is dead; but his death must be concealed. Fielding and Ralph climb up to the saint's tomb and are attacked by bees. Fielding and Aziz meet: Fielding is taut in manner, Aziz 'impertinent'. Fielding's explanation of the misunderstanding does not appease Aziz. He clings to the new life he has built himself: he had built it on a mistake, but it was to him fundamentally satisfying and correct. Memories of Mrs Moore and Fielding's marriage to her daughter trouble this obduracy.

pujah See note p. 61.
the tank i.e. lake or reservoir.

Chapter 36, Water festival

The revelation – of the divine birth – has come and gone; but the effects remain. Aziz rides out of the town, on the way meeting Godbole, who assures him that, he is, 'as far as my limitations permit, your true friend'. (He had known the truth about Fielding's marriage.) The 'moment of the Despised and Rejected' arrives. Aziz looks down with scorn and anger on the Guest House boat, in which Fielding, his wife and Ralph are proceeding to watch the torchlight procession. He passes, in the quiet Indian evening, to the Guest House. He reads two letters that he finds lying on the piano. He is oppressed and angered by their atmosphere of easy intimacy, between man and woman and between Fielding and Ronny. Ralph enters; not the usual imperial type. He feels Aziz's hostility and cruelty. As Aziz relents, Ralph senses this, too; and Aziz experiences again the sympathetic call of one person to another that he had experienced with the boy's mother, Mrs Moore.

He recoils from the pattern of the past; he fears that the cycle of 'mosque, caves, mosque, caves' – of intimacy leading to disaster – is beginning again. But 'his heart was too full to draw back'. They row on the lake and see the chhatri of the Rajah's father – Ralph had led them to the one point from which it could be seen – and Aziz hears the chant of 'Esmiss Esmoor' mingling with the chant of 'Radhakrishna'. Their boat collides with Fielding's. They capsize; the tray containing the image of the village of Gokul is scattered on the waters. Thunder peals, and the 'great blur of the last twenty-four hours' draws to its close.

Note the words that describe this climax: 'desultory', 'ragged', 'unsatisfactory', 'undramatic'. Here is the confusion, the lack of definition and clarity that is characteristic of India and of the situation there, a situation of imperialism and alien rule. In this confusion and becoming part of it Aziz and Fielding make spiritual contact once more.

Radhakrishna Krishna an incarnation of Vishnu; Rhada his consort.
chhatri Canopy (underneath which the image of the Rajah rests).
Ganpati One of the many names of Ganasa, the eldest son of Siva.
bunderbust Arrangement, disposition, revenue. Used colloquially here, (meaning 'to make a mess of things').

Chapter 37, 'No, not yet . . . No, not there'

The Guest House party is departing on the morrow. Fielding, who does not 'travel as lightly as in the past', discovers the facts about the King-Emperor George the Fifth High School. Aziz and Fielding ride 'between jolly bushes and rocks', in countryside that is 'as parklike as England' but, nevertheless, 'queer'. Fielding speaks of his marriage, of the way his wife, Stella, has ideas that he does not share, and of how the visit to Mau has somehow soothed her, brought her some kind of solution and has also 'blessed' their union. The mishap on the lake and the whole context of incidents involved with this has brought Aziz some kind of peace, too: he will write to Miss Quested and tell her that he realizes, now, how brave she was. (The episode of the caves is over, at last.)

But he withdraws from the kind of intimacy that Fielding offers. He realizes, as does Fielding, that this is their 'last free intercourse' (good-bye): they have no social meeting-place. They wrangle about politics – confident in their deep personal friendship. Fielding mocks India's nationalist ambitions. Aziz, successfully rearing his horse, cries out his hatred for the English; some time, however long it will be, 'we shall drive every blasted Englishman into the sea'. The novel moves to its climax. When this is done, then, says Aziz fiercely, 'you and I shall be friends'. Fielding pleads that they can be friends now. But this is not so. Everything else that is there says 'No'. Their horses swerve apart.

the Caaba of Union The Caaba is an oblong stone building within the great mosque of Mecca – the house of God. Union implies harmony with God.
the thorn bushes An image, it seems, of the harsh world.
the Friend An image of God.
Saivite temple Temple to Siva, the Hindu god. He represents both the destructive and the reproductive powers of nature.

Revision questions of Part 3

1 Describe the air of confusion, jollity and devotion that attends the religious celebration at Mau.
2 What further evidence do we now find of the change in Aziz?
3 What part does Mrs Moore play in the closing stages of the novel?
4 What changes are evident in Fielding?
5 Describe precisely and thoughtfully the course and the changing nature of 'the last free intercourse' between Aziz and Fielding.

General questions

1 'A novel about race relationships.' Does this seem to you an adequate description of *A Passage to India*?

2 Show how symbols state and reinforce the meanings of the novel.

3 'A novel without a hero.' Do you agree with this comment on *A Passage to India*?

4 Discuss the social comedy of the novel.

5 'A novel about places.' How illuminating do you find this comment?

6 From your reading of *A Passage to India* would you say that Forster lacks passion?

7 Several critics have felt that Mrs Moore is a flaw, a weakness in the novel. Consider the grounds of their objection and then state your own feelings on this point.

8 'Both Fielding and Aziz are drawn with tenderness but also with an unsparing honesty of insight.' Discuss.

9 'One is disappointed finally in the novel, for neither Aziz nor Fielding lives up to one's expectations.' Do *you* feel this sense of disappointment?

10 How important do you think Professor Godbole is in the novel?

11 What impression of British officials and British officialdom in India do you get from Forster's novel?

12 Show how the novel contains several minor characters who are briefly but precisely shown.

13 'An air of frustration and confusion pervades the whole novel.' Discuss.

14 'One forgets that these people are of different races and one sees them simply as individuals struggling to "connect" with each other.' Do you agree?

15 'The main characters are never free agents but are dominated by the pressure of circumstances, of environment, of India.' Discuss.

16 'Forster simply depicts; he never passes judgement.' Do you agree?

17 'A powerful sense of evil dominates the novel.' Discuss.

18 'Forster repeatedly makes one aware of the limited scope of his novel, that it does not set out to deal with all humanity but with a part of it only.' Discuss.

19 'One is finally left with a feeling of intense pessimism.' Is this the feeling *A Passage to India* evokes in you?

20 On what grounds would you recommend anyone to read *A Passage to India*?